THE BIBLE
FOR EVERYONE

Virginia Mary Heffernan

THE BRUCE PUBLISHING COMPANY / *Milwaukee*

NIHIL OBSTAT:

Richard J. Sklba, S.S.L., S.T.D.
Censor librorum

IMPRIMATUR:

✠ William E. Cousins
Archbishop of Milwaukee
July, 5, 1968

The Old Testament excerpts used in this book are from *The Jerusalem Bible,* copyright © 1966 by Darton, Longman and Todd, Ltd., and Doubleday Company, Inc. Reprinted by permission of the publishers.

The New Testament excerpts are taken from *The New Testament* translated by James A. Kleist, S.J. and Joseph L. Lilly, C.M., copyright © 1956 by The Bruce Publishing Company.

Library of Congress Catalog Card Number: 68–54986

Copyright © 1969 The Bruce Publishing Company

MADE IN THE UNITED STATES OF AMERICA

To my Mother,
whose desire to understand life
has been whetted by faith and experience

Introduction

This book offers a rapid survey of the highlights of both the Old and New Testaments. Its purpose is, on the one hand, to give a general idea of the contents of the Bible and, on the other, to relate the message of the Bible to contemporary concerns. I have written it for people who are growing and are wise enough to know that they have a long way to go, and I have tried to make the presentation "popular." Thus the book is not intended to be an authoritative, scholarly study. Nonetheless, the book does try to conform to the general ideas taught by contemporary biblical scholars, and reminders are scattered throughout the book to the effect that its stories and events must not be read literally: the events we find in the Bible were selected and interpreted by the biblical writers in such a way as to reveal the acts of God to peoples who lived long ago. Thus the ideas of the Bible are expressed in a manner that was intelligible to them, but they may not be clear to us. And, as a matter of fact, what we call "literally true" is not free of interpretation. Our ideas about what is important and accurate are not the last or only word on the subject of truth. *Time* magazine has as developed and specialized a "literary genre" as does the Bible.

Let's take an example. If we say that somebody walked for forty days we mean that we can tick off the days he was walking on a calendar and count them and we will come out with the number forty. But supposing we were more interested in what was happening in the human soul and what God was doing to a man — the number of calendar days he walked somewhere would not be worth recording. What would be worth recording? His sincerity. The completeness of his conversion to God. Now the biblical peoples associated forty years with the complete replacement of one gen-

[v]

eration of peoples by another. Thus forty days, forty years and multiples of forty like 400 might have been merely convenient ways of saying "complete" and "complete change."

I hope this example gives you the idea that the Bible cannot be read literally, that is, with our meaning applied to all its details. Neither can we say the Bible is lying if it says 400 years passed when we can prove from archaeology that 430 years passed, or that the mustard seed is the littlest when we can show some smaller seeds exist, and other things of that sort. When the Bible says that Eve was made from Adam's rib it is saying, in a way perfectly clear to the people for whom the story was written, that Eve is like Adam and meant to be his companion. In fact, the meaning of the imagery of the rib is explained a few sentences after the picture-story in the Bible text. The first chapters of the Bible are theology and not merely history which can be compared for "accuracy" with the theory of evolution. We have to escape from our narrow idea of reality in order to read the Bible. Even if this were all we got out of reading the Bible it would be worth the effort.

However, you and I should be able to get more out of the Bible than a bit of thought-freedom. Yes, open your mind. Yes, loosen up your imagination. But then, think about what is said and even about my suggestions (which I think you will find fairly easy to distinguish from the text itself) and look for God's revelation of Himself to mankind. Try to understand what the human-divine relationship means. Try to come face to face with the God who made you in His image.

Preface

Jesus proclaimed the coming on earth of the Kingdom of God. He, Himself, fulfilled the scriptural hope for a Messiah, or Savior, sent by God to reconcile mankind. The progressive development of revelation began with the first man and assumed a dimension of increased depth through Israel's historical passage. It was completed by Jesus. Does this mean that human personal and social growth stopped with Jesus? Let's review a bit and see if we can figure out an answer to this question.

The greatness of God, and of creation as His act, was somehow revealed to the first ancestors of all mankind. Then God united a people set apart to be another more conscious and explicit sign of His activity. He gave His people an identity and unity, uniting them in the beginning through the promise of a fruitful land in which to live. He gave His people a task to perform as a service to all mankind. The Hebrew identity may be hard to pin down, but you and I can look at it from an American viewpoint: we look to results. The Jews have accompanied the Christians throughout Christian history and have never lost their identity although they have been persecuted, executed and scattered over the face of the earth. This people of God remains a powerful sign of the incompleteness of human reconciliation, the other side, so to speak, or a sign of the underlying tension within Christian hope. They remain significant — that is, a sign fact — as a part of that community having faith in the one transcendent God.

What were the major steps in the growth of revelation? God began tutoring mankind at the beginning of its evolution. As consciousness began to disentangle itself from nature, He began His explicit revelation. Remember that Moses lived during the late bronze age. Much later, when mankind had command of writing, knowledge about God was written down in what we call the scriptures, or writings. The earliest texts of the Bible were written during the tenth or eleventh centuries before Christ. At that time the authors of the first five books pulled together a variety of old stories, traditional laws and rituals to make God better understood by the people of their own time. They re-interpreted and co-ordinated what had already been learned about God's relationship with mankind. What they wrote is theology, not history as we understand history to be.

The understanding of God and man grew gradually more profound. Each event in the history of the chosen people of God added a new dimension to divine revelation. New authors wrote, or revised, the old writings about the acts of God. The idea of the kingdom grew deeper when the Israelites became a kingdom. Individual morality, that is, personal trust in God, was better and better understood, but never separated from the life of the whole people and their collective destiny. Some of the power and perennial beauty of the Bible lies in this progressive comprehensiveness, this unity of physical creation, social existence and personal consciousness in a single advancing synthesis.

The orginal promise was relatively limited to man's material needs and bodily existence, and came at a time in history when technology permitted few other preoccupations. The later prophets were involved with social history. They spoke about the public events in which they participated, and, speaking about these events with the authority of God, they exposed spiritual dimensions hidden in the more earthly original promises. The prophets spiritualized the promise.

A literature of human wisdom also accumulated. This was collected in various books of sayings, poems, and songs, that balance the divine zeal of the prophets with "common sense" and human warmth. The wisdom books, which now form part of the Bible, humanized the promise.

Some men of genius sought answers to questions which arose with the increase of leisure and vocabulary for human reflection. They illustrated moral themes in story form. Thus we read in the Bible about the uprightness of Esther, Judith and Tobias. A soul-searching drama about the problem of evil was written. In this

book, the Book of Job, the dimensions of the problem of the suffering of the good man were explored, but the question was not
"answered." Instead, the disproportion between human understanding and the vast power of God was simply accepted. THE BIBLE FOR
EVERYONE passes over these parts of the Bible very quickly, leaving you much room for exploration. The coming of Jesus gave another answer to the question suffering poses to any temporally-
oriented causal morality. He bridged the distance between man and
God without diminishing the importance of temporal morality. Job
could not say that the suffering of the good man had value, but
only that the God of all creation must be trusted no matter what
happened. Jesus declared that such suffering had value. He became
a living sign of its value by returning to life through suffering and
death. However, Jesus did not "answer" the question the way we
incline to want it to be answered. He did not do away with suffering. Jesus' answer has many sides to it, but one of its aspects is
that it opens life to further growth, especially to an appreciation of
the universality of suffering and of the human power to grow toward God through suffering. He emphasized the moral act, rather
than worldly consequences. Jesus, who fulfilled both the spiritual
and human necessities of the promise, brought men and women
a new life in truth and freedom, beyond the sinfulness and evil to
which they were formerly enslaved.

Do you still remember the question we asked at the beginning
of this summary? It was about the progressive development of the
human-divine relationship. Did Jesus' fulfillment of God's promise
to His people put an end to progress? If all that is recorded in the
Old Testament led to Him, what next?

The answer is that growth and the progressive refinement of
mankind did not stop with Jesus but it became different. A new
creation began with Jesus, who is often called the new Adam. Paul
told his friends: "You have stripped off your old behavior with your
old self, and you have put on a new self which will progress toward
true knowledge the more it is renewed in the image of its creator."
He goes on to explain that this means growth in the true image of
God which is found in Christ Jesus.

In the New Testament as in the Old there is a human work to
be done: the preaching of the Good News to every creature, both

by individuals and by the visible collectivity of the people of God. The plan is not all laid out, but is a seed that must grow. Further fulfillment is still expected when the Lord will come again, but no one knows its day or hour in history. Meanwhile, the Lord Jesus is with us as the first born of a new people being formed in God's image through the Spirit until the redemption of all creation is given to a human race which has completed its work, which is, as Paul wrote: filling up what is lacking in Christ.

Contents

[xi]

CONTENTS

PART TWO: THE NEW TESTAMENT

PART ONE:
THE OLD TESTAMENT

PART ONE:
THE OLD TESTAMENT

1. The First Acts of God

The Bible begins with the life-giving activity of God. On the first page God is pictured creating the main features of the world. Here is how the Old Testament starts:

> In the beginning God created the heavens and the earth. Now the earth was a formless void, there was darkness over the deep, and God's spirit hovered over the water.
>
> Gen 1:1–2

From these few words we learn basic facts about God. God is not a mere natural force, personifying the sun or the sea, or some animal or place. He is not like the nature gods people worshipped in those ancient times when this part of the Bible was written. But *God is independent of the natural world.* Before Him there was no natural world at all. Nor was there any "before" God.

This idea is not so easy to express. How would you describe the untouchable, unheard of absence of everything? Think a minute. Do you have your "picture" of nothingness? Now try to imagine darkness over a nameless, bottomless deep. The Hebrew biblical writer did get the idea across, didn't he? There was nothing until God thought of things and gave them reality. The Bible continues:

> God said, 'Let there be light,' and there was light. God saw that light was good, and God divided light from darkness. God called light 'day,' and darkness he called 'night'. Evening came and morning came: the first day.
>
> Gen 1:3–2:3 (selected)

Notice that, with the succession of evening and morning, what we call "time" came into being. The sun, which our science tells us causes day (along with the rotation of the earth), is not created

[3]

until the fourth day in the biblical account. But ancient peoples did not have the picture we have of the physical universe; they thought the earth was covered by a great dome, or vault, which contained the sun and moon and stars, and opened from time to time to let rain down from above the vault. Our expression for a big storm, "the heavens opened," reflects this ancient idea.

God said, 'Let there be a vault in the waters to divide the water in two. . . . ' God called the vault 'heaven'. Evening came and morning came: the second day.

God said, 'Let the waters under heaven come together into a single mass, and let dry land appear.' And so it was . . . . and God saw that it was good.

God said, 'Let the earth produce vegetation: seed-bearing plants and fruit trees bearing fruit with their seed inside . . . ' the third day.

God said, 'Let there be lights in the vault of heaven to divide day from night. . . . ' And so it was. God made the two great lights: the greater light to govern the day, the smaller light to govern the night, and the stars. God set them in the vault of heaven to shine on the earth . . . . the fourth day.

God said, 'Let the waters teem with living creatures, and let birds fly above the earth. . . . ' God saw that it was good. God blessed them, saying, 'Be fruitful, multiply . . . ' . . . the fifth day.

God said 'Let the earth produce every kind of living creature: cattle, reptiles and every kind of wild beast'. . . . God saw that it was good.

God said, 'Let us make man in our own image, in the likeness of ourselves, and let them be masters of the fish of the sea, the birds of heaven, the cattle, all the wild beasts and all the reptiles that crawl upon the earth.' . . . . God saw all he had made, and indeed it was very good. Evening came and morning came: the sixth day.

. . . On the seventh day God completed the work he had been doing. He rested on the seventh day . . .

Gen 1:3–2:2

Dots in the text above indicate that words have been left out. If you have a Bible handy why not read the whole text, which is about twice as long as this quote? It is very majestic in its entirety and has a quiet joy and awe-fulness. Then you can see how excitingly bold God was, as the Poet Blake did when he wrote his poem about just one animal, the tiger: "What immortal hand or eye dared frame thy fearful symmetry?" How many and how marvelous are the creatures God has made! But before we go on to the creatures God made, let us see what else we have learned about God from this narrative.

How did God create? He acted in a personal way. He decided. He commanded. What He commanded was done. And then He reflected on His work. He saw that it was good. It had value. God was satisfied with the worth of the work He had begun to do. The Bible shows us that *God is a person.*

Of course, this personal activity of God, which is described as similar to the personal activity of men, is also very different from human personal behavior. The biblical author does not make God in the image of man, but the other way round: man is the image of, or somehow like, God. It is important to understand this, because many people have been confused about God's personal appearance in the Bible and have said that men invented God in the image of man. The Hebrews weren't confused. They had a clear concept of God's much more than human powers.

God would not be God if He were not personal, for He is deeply concerned with every dimension or part of His work. If God were merely in command of nature and not also in command of what we know intimately as ourselves — "persons," and the experience of consciousness — God would be incomplete. He would not be God of *everything.* Neither could we love Him.

The Bible shows us that God, who in Himself is altogether "other," usually relates to every dimension of His creation according to the nature or reality proper to that part of what He has made. But He *can* relate to anything as He pleases. He can cause the sea to divide, the sun to stand still, life to return to the dead, and even come Himself to live as one of this human race He created.

God's relations with mankind are fitted to the being He has given to man: both to the individual person with unique interior growth, and to man as social. God made men capable of knowing Him, of coming to know Him better, and of choosing to follow Him. He speaks to each of us individually through what we call our conscience. He speaks to us through the other men with whom we live and from whom we learn. He is present through all human works: languages, the accumulating of knowledge, the making of history and the collective subduing of the earth.

So far we have only looked at the first chapter of the Bible, where the story of creation is fitted into a week. The week is not a natural division of time, but a human invention which many great civilizations, such as the Chinese, have not had. It is a device by which society is organized; the biblical author used the week to organize this story of creation and introduce the entire Bible.

The "days" description of creation is followed immediately by another, believed by scholars to be the older of the two. The second creation story is not organized by days and concentrates more on man than on the cosmos. This repeating of stories, which occurs over and over in the Bible, teaches us a third fact about God. *God cannot be captured in any one expression.* Neither is He made known all at once. He becomes better known.

All through the Bible its many authors were inspired to add new ideas about God's activity of creation. For example, John tells us that Jesus once said:

> I am the light of the world;
> anyone who follows me will not be walking in the dark;
> he will have the light of life.
>
> Jn 8:12

These words unite Jesus with the creative work of God described at the beginning of the Bible as the making of light and life.

Among the beautiful poems in the book of Psalms, there are several reviews of God's creative work that were meant to be sung to the accompaniment of guitar-like instruments. One of these is numbered Psalm 148 and has the title "Cosmic Hymn of Praise" in the Jerusalem edition of the Bible. "Yahweh," an ancient Hebrew proper name for God, is used in this poem. That all things created are *not* God, but exist only because of God's creative activity is beautifully expressed. How we wish we had the lost music to complete the joyfulness of these praises!

[6]

Cosmic hymn of praise

Alleluia!

Let heaven praise Yahweh:
praise him, heavenly heights,
praise him, all his angels,
praise him, all his armies!

Praise him, sun and moon,
praise him, shining stars,
praise him, highest heavens,
and waters above the heavens!

Let them all praise the name of Yahweh,
at whose command they were created;
he has fixed them in their place for ever,
by an unalterable statute.

Let earth praise Yahweh:
sea-monsters and all the deeps,
fire and hail, snow and mist,
gales that obey his decree,

mountains and hills,
orchards and forests,
wild animals, and farm animals,
snakes and birds,

all kings on earth and nations,
princes, all rulers in the world,
young men and girls,
old people, and children too!

Let them all praise the name of Yahweh,
for his name and no other is sublime,
transcending earth and heaven in majesty,
raising the fortunes of his people,
to the praises of the devout,
of Israel, the people dear to him.

Ps 148

2. The Making of Mankind

Man is made in the image of God. There can be no doubt that this is the key biblical thought about man. As you read the Bible you will meet it again and again:

> God said, 'Let us make man in our own image, in the likeness of ourselves . . .'
> God created man in the image of himself,
> in the image of God he created him,
> male and female he created them.
>
> Gen 1:26, 27
> On the day God created Adam he made him in the likeness of God. Male and female he created them. He blessed them and gave them the name 'Man' on the day they were created.
>
> Gen 5:2

If men had not been created in the image of God, then Jesus' command to men, "You must therefore be perfect just as your heavenly Father is perfect," would not make much sense. But Jesus did say this, and could say this, because a basic likeness to God is in man already.

"Likeness" is a double meaning word. It does not mean exact "sameness." Men are not the same as God, only partly the same and partly different. Men do not create as God does: they may reach the moon but they did not make it. In what way are man and God alike? How do you think they are alike?

First, and most important, *man and God can communicate*. The whole Bible is itself a divine-human dialogue. Sometimes this dialogue between God and man is put into words. But more often it is expressed in action. God and man *do* things which relate them to each other. These doings accumulate as a history.

[8]

In Jesus Christ the dialogue between God and man is without flaw or defect. All men are caught up together in Jesus' perfect conversation with God, which was in words:

'Father, I thank you for hearing my prayer.
I knew indeed that you always hear me,
but I speak
for the sake of all these who stand round me.'

Jn 11:41–42

and action:

'. . . I do nothing of myself:
what the Father has taught me
is what I preach;
he who sent me is with me,
and has not left me to myself,
for I always do what pleases him.'

Jn 8:28–29

How did the ancient Hebrew authors of the Old Testament convey this idea of divine-human likeness as a capacity for dialogue? Very simply. They recorded conversations between God and men. Adam and Eve talked with God. So did Abraham and Moses and many other friends of God whom we shall meet in the Bible.

This talking together is not the only human "likeness" to God, even with respect to words. For God brought all His other creatures to man to be named by him. Thus *God gave man a share in His work of creation,* which, if you remember, is described as speaking: "God said . . . and so it was." Ancient people were not afraid to affirm that they were radically different from animals and other creatures because of their ability to use words or languages. Some modern people, who profit from what mankind has accomplished with his unique gift of language, are less willing than the Hebrews to find themselves different from animals. Maybe these moderns are embarrassed to be so like God, knowing their weaknesses and frailties also. This creative activity of naming and thus knowing the creatures of God is still being done by scientists who constantly discover more and more parts of creation to name.

Closely connected with the naming of creatures is the mastery of creatures. As God is master of all creation, so man is "like" God as having charge of creatures:

[9]

'Be fruitful, multiply, fill the earth and conquer it. Be masters of the fish of the sea, the birds of heaven and all living animals on the earth'.

Gen 1:28

But this command to care for creation was given to mankind in Eden, which is a way of saying that it is proper to perfect human life. After men disrupted Eden's harmony (according to the biblical way of explaining life) God punished men by making the earth and creatures resistant to human control. We know that the earth resists human control. Gradually, through long centuries of effort and with the help of God, men have regained some of their mastery of creation. This is one aspect of the restoration of "likeness" to God. And restoration of the human likeness to God is what the Bible is all about.

How else is man made in the image of God? Remember what we have learned about God. God is independent of His creation. In naming and mastering creatures *man is partly independent of nature,* as God is fully independent. Through an independence similar to God's creative speaking men can master creatures, manipulate them, and use them.

To use and direct creatures men must choose. They must value various things more than others. They must have purposes. These human abilities are called moral. All these capacities for knowing and acting and moral choice are what make people persons. *Human beings are persons* in the image of the personal God of the Bible.

Of course, you know that you are a person when you think about yourself. Being "you" is more real than a list like "having knowledge, holding values, deciding on goals." *You* can't be summed up in words. You express yourself by all your reactions to people and by what you do: by speaking or being silent, by dancing and becoming skilled in sports, by writing poems or acting in plays, by drawing or dressing yourself in some style of clothes, by praying and by helping other people. But you know that, while all these things express *you,* none of them is the whole *you,* for *you are a person, made in the image of God and like God always more than any single expression, or even all expressions put together.*

[10]

3. The Human Problem

Have you ever done anything you really didn't want to do? I'll bet you can remember some unhappy, being-separated-from-yourself experiences. Paul did. He mentioned this common misery in his letter to the Roman Christians:

> I cannot understand my own behavior. I fail to carry out the things I want to do, and I find myself doing the very things I hate.
>
> Rom 7:15

From this kind of experience we all know that there is something the matter within ourselves. Our friends admit that they have inner troubles, too. Much of literature is about internal human discord, and helps us to understand human problems. Whether we study a little history, or read the daily newspaper, or watch T.V., we learn about wars and murders and deceits, poverty and the failures of science, medicine, agriculture and commerce. We encounter evil, defiling God's image in mankind, at every street corner.

Do you admire people like Anne Frank, who are overwhelmed, but hold onto a deep faith in mankind? Most people do. Most people long for the happiness of human harmony. But they are very, very discouraged by the shabby sinfulness they meet instead.

The Bible takes a positive stand about all this misery. It tells us that God meant mankind to live harmoniously. God's works are creative and good. Man is meant to join in this good creative activity of God. But to go against God is destructive. This is what mankind has done and continues to do.

The word "Adam" is used two ways in the Bible. Sometimes it is the proper name of the first man. But it is also a collective noun which means "man" or "mankind." In the latter part of the second creation story you can see that Adam is living in a society which already has customs and ways of doing things. This description of man's nature supposes a culture in which nomadic shepherds, farmers and townspeople meet. Whether we think of Adam as an individual or as mankind, we learn about the positive side of human nature from the description of Adam's creation, and we learn about the negative side of man from the story of the fall.

The story of Adam's sin is a description of mankind's refusal of God, or better, of mankind's refusal to accept limits to his God-like qualities of independence and personal freedom. It can be read as "original" and it can be read as happening here and now in me and in you. It is a factual description of what man finds himself to be. The Bible does not look back to satisfy us with reasons for the way things are, but begins with the way things are and describes them so we can learn how things should be and act accordingly.

The marvelous news with which the Bible begins and with which it reaches a climax in the Good News, or Gospels, is that the unhappy negative condition of man is against God's will. Men *do* go against God, but this is a wrong which God and man together are gradually making right. The making right is in human fashion, through the use of human abilities. God's guidance is normally a guidance of these abilities: of the free mind and the full moral person. Jesus was the first man to overcome "the world" of sinfulness and make completely right the human relationship with God.

How does the story of man go? God made man of dust from the soil, and gave him a breath of life. What does that tell us? That man is related to earth but also has invisible spiritual qualities.

God put mankind in the garden of Eden to cultivate and care for it. Eden is pictured as an oasis in the desert; it is called paradise in many translations. What matters, however, is God's command to care for paradise. God made man active and gave him a work to do.

God said, "It is not good that man should be alone." He brought man all the animals but man found no companion among them. He found himself to be different from the animals. So God made woman to be the companion of man. The unity of man and woman is expressed in the mythological image of taking a rib from man and making it into a woman. Man recognizes immediately:

'This at last is bone from my bones,
and flesh from my flesh!
This is to be called woman,
for this was taken from man.'

This is why a man leaves his father and mother and joins
himself to his wife, and they become one body.

Gen 2:23–24

The family is basic to society. Man is mean to live in the unity of
marriage and, leaving the union of his parents, to form his own
lasting relationship with a woman he loves.

Yes, but what about the trees and the serpent, which seem so
absurd to many people. Do they seem absurd to you? Probably
they do, for we have developed a keen awareness of absurdity, all
sorts of absurdities.

If you read the Bible text you may notice that there are two
trees: one symbolic of the moral order, the tree of the knowledge
of good and evil; and one symbolic of eternal life. The trees the
ancient desert peoples knew outlived them and brought them fruits
like olives and dates by which they lived, so it was natural for them
to symbolize immortality in this way, by a tree. What is unusual
and peculiar to the Bible is the other tree. The Hebrews were not
so concerned with the tree of life, for life was in the hands of God.
They were more concerned about the other tree and the practical
problem it represents.

In the biblical picture-story of the human problem the serpent (a
creature worshipped as a god of fertility and thus an idol opposed
to the true God and a symbol of evil) suggests to the woman that
God has not been perfectly honest, and was preventing mankind
from being like God by forbidding them to eat of the tree of good
and evil. He makes disobedience to God look good rather than evil.
The obvious attractiveness of the tree supports his suggestion. Isn't
this what leads to sin every day — that some evil act looks good for
the moment?

Eve's husband was with her but he said nothing, letting her try
first. She did. She then gave him some of the fruit and he ate it.
"Then the eyes of both of them were opened and they realised that
they were naked." What before had been normal suddenly embarrassed them: they had distanced themselves from the good.

[13]

Adam and Eve hid from the God. But God called out to them. He questioned them. Their answers were no better and no worse than the excuses I'll bet you've heard a thousand times. Real "He did it-s." Eve blamed the serpent and Adam blamed Eve. What would God have done if they had honestly admitted their sin? But they didn't.

God ignored their excuses and accusations. He punished the serpent, Eve, and Adam, each in turn. His punishments are central to the life situations of each of the human partners: pain in childbearing is multiplied for the woman, while the man is to suffer in his work of providing food for his family. The social discord between husbands and wives is also brought out by the biblical passage: while the woman, with a deep tenderness, is devoted to her husband, he lords it over her. Finally, their spiritual breath will leave their earthly bodies and they will die.

Then it is said that God made clothes for them to wear. Why did God do that? Was He starting them out in the industriousness by which mankind has slowly regained control of himself and the earth, so that today he has somewhat mitigated the pains of childbirth and the labor of tilling the soil? Perhaps. Or was God simply demonstrating His graciousness, as Jesus did much later, after His resurrection, when He made a fire ready on the shore of Galilee, so the apostles (who had deserted Him when He was crucified) could fry their breakfast fish?

In any case, God expelled mankind from paradise. After their expulsion the biblical account brings in, one by one, the corruptions of mankind. First there was a murder: Cain murdered his brother Abel. Then there was unlimited polygamy and more murders. Fewer and fewer men spoke with God. Finally there was so much wickedness that God regretted having made man on the earth. How very terrible men must have become! Yet one solitary witness to God's goodness remained.

4. Noah and the First of Many New Beginnings

Mankind had become completely corrupt. Nonetheless, God found one good man on earth. His name was Noah. One of the most picturesque stories in the Bible is the story of the flood with which God destroyed all men and beasts, saving only Noah's family and with him two of each species to repopulate the earth.

God said to Noah, 'The end has come for all things of flesh; I have decided this, because the earth is full of violence of man's making, and I will efface them from the earth. Make yourself an ark out of resinous wood. Make it with reeds and line it with pitch inside and out. . . .

'For my part I mean to bring a flood, and send the waters over the earth, to destroy all flesh on it, every living creature under heaven; everything on earth shall perish. But I will establish my Covenant with you, and you must go on board the ark, yourself, your sons, your wife, and your sons' wives along with you. From all living creatures, from all flesh, you must take two of each kind aboard the ark, to save their lives with yours; they must be a male and a female. Of every kind of bird, of every kind of animal and of every kind of reptile on the ground, two must go with you so that their lives may be saved. For your part provide yourself with eatables of all kinds, and lay in a store of them, to serve as food for yourself and them.' Noah did this; he did all that God had ordered him. . . .

That very day Noah and his sons Shem, Ham and Japheth boarded the ark, with Noah's wife and the three wives of his sons, and with them wild beasts of every kind, cattle of every kind, reptiles of every kind that crawls on the earth, birds of every kind, all that flies, everything with wings. One pair of all that is flesh and has the breath of life boarded the ark with Noah; and so there went in a male and a female of every creature that is flesh, just as God had ordered him.

And Yahweh closed the door behind Noah.

The flood lasted forty days on the earth. The waters swelled, lifting the ark until it was raised above the earth. The waters rose and swelled greatly on the earth, and the ark sailed on the waters. The waters rose more and more on the earth so that all the highest mountains under the whole of heaven were submerged.

Rain ceased to fall from heaven; the waters gradually ebbed from the earth. After a hundred and fifty days the waters fell, and in the seventh month, on the seventeenth day of that month, the ark came to rest on the mountains of Ararat. The water gradually fell until the tenth month when, on the first day of the tenth month, the mountain peaks appeared.

At the end of forty days Noah opened the porthole he had made in the ark and he sent out the raven. This went off, and flew back and forth until the water dried up from the earth. Then he sent out the dove, to see whether the waters were receding from the surface of the earth. The dove, finding nowhere to perch, returned to him in the ark, for there was water over the whole surface of the earth; putting out his hand he took hold of it and brought it back into the ark with him. After waiting seven more days, again he sent out the dove from the ark. In the evening, the dove came back to him and there it was with a new olive-branch in its beak. So Noah realised that the waters were receding from the earth.

Gen 6:13–8:11 (selected)

After the flood was over Noah's first act was to offer thanks to God. God was pleased. For a sign of His acceptance God put a rainbow in the sky. Rainbows still appear when storms are over to remind men that it is God who restores the sunshine and makes the earth fruitful. Don't you find that rainbows cheer you up?

What was God's understanding with Noah? God agreed never again to destroy the earth, but to maintain its orderly natural processes forever. God did not require mankind to be without defects. Noah was a good man but he was not perfect: he was the first to cultivate grapes and produce wine, and got quite drunk on the wine. This led his son Ham to sin, also.

God asked men to realistically recognize their dependence and inadequacy. God reminded Noah of the work He had given Adam to do on this earth. It is man's responsibility to be fruitful, multiply, teem over the earth and be lord of it. The word we use for this today is "development." To develop the earth is a work which God has charged man to carry out. When and where it is not well done the pains with which God punished mankind are very much in evidence: malnutrition, disease, social disorder and war. Man — all men of all societies together — has the responsibility to do away with these ills.

5. God's Promise to Abraham and his Family

The Hebrew patriarchs, Abraham, Isaac, Jacob and his son Joseph, lived between 2000 and 1700 B.C. That's nearly 4,000 years ago. The biblical stories about these men and their families were retold for centuries before they were first written down in the tenth century before Christ Jesus. Why were these stories remembered for such a very long time?

The Bible tells us that the events these stories record have universal meaning. God blessed Abraham (at the beginning of the story of the chosen family, before his name, Abram, had been changed to Abraham) saying:

> All the tribes of the earth shall bless themselves by you.
> Gen 12:3

Isn't this the way all blessings are brought to mankind? Do not all inventions and social ideas originate with single men and women of genius? Are we not blessed by the unknown inventors of the needle, the hoe, and the wheel, by Marconi, Edison and Einstein, by Socrates, Shakespeare and Elizabeth Browning, by Galen and Dr. Salk — surely you can make your own long list. Did not Columbus go on a long journey into the unknown and begin a vast migration? Nonetheless, the blessings brought to mankind through God's instrument, Abraham, are different from all others for they have to do directly with the return of mankind to God. To this Hebrew family God reveals Himself; through this family He tutors all mankind. God's chosen people never lose their timeliness.

God said to Abram, "Leave your country, your family and your

[18]

father's house, for the land I will show you." "Going forth" is something God demands of His chosen friends. Jesus repeatedly asked people to leave everything they possessed to follow Him, and some of His harshest words have this theme: hate your father and your mother; let the dead bury the dead. The following of God demands an absolute cutting loose from old ties and obligations. The Bible constantly contrasts fidelity and infidelity to God in this way.

However, loving God is not a matter of simply leaving home. It is a matter of faith. It is a matter of conversion. Paul talked about Abraham very often, always in order to teach the same idea:

> It was by faith that Abraham obeyed the call to set out for a country that was the inheritance given to him and his descendants, and that he set out without knowing where he was going. By faith he arrived, as a foreigner, in the Promised Land, and lived there as if in a strange country, with Isaac and Jacob, who were heirs with him of the same promise. They lived there in tents while he looked forward to a city founded, designed and built by God.
>
> Heb 11:8–10

Abram left his homeland when God told him to go. He was an old man, seventy-five, according to the biblical record written more than a thousand years later. He took his wife, Sarai, his nephew, Lot, and the entire pastoral peoples and possessions he had in his care. We would describe him as the chief of a nomadic tribe.

The first flowering of civilization had recently withered in Mesopotamia. This was the land he left. He went westward to Palestine, or the country of Israel, which was then called Canaan. God appeared to Abram in Canaan and promised him: "It is to your descendants that I will give this land." How did Abram react? He built an altar to God at the place where this promise was made to him, but moved on. He had always to move on seeking pasture lands for his flocks. Because of a famine he went all the way to Egypt, the center of another great ancient civilization.

The next incident in the story of Abram seems curious to us. Here was God's chosen man: what did he do? He told a lie! And why? Because he was afraid of being killed. Was not God with him everywhere he went, protecting him? Yes, but he was afraid. Abram was not perfect, and he fell into sin through fear, as did

[19]

Peter long centuries after his time. Faith is believing that God will do what He has promised. Even the men who are examples of faith in the Bible sometimes act like men without faith. There is a gap between their merits and the work God does for them and through them. Here is the story of Abram's lie:

> When famine came to the land Abram went down into Egypt to stay there for the time, since the land was hard pressed by the famine. On the threshold of Egypt he said to his wife Sarai, 'Listen! I know you are a beautiful woman. When the Egyptians see you they will say, "That is his wife", and they will kill me but spare you. Tell them you are my sister, so that they may treat me well because of you and spare my life out of regard for you.' When Abram arrived in Egypt the Egyptians did indeed see that the woman was very beautiful. When Pharaoh's officials saw her they sang her praises to Pharaoh and the woman was taken into Pharaoh's palace. He treated Abram well because of her, and he received flocks, oxen, donkeys, men and women slaves, she-donkeys and camels. But Yahweh inflicted severe plagues on Pharaoh and his household because of Abram's wife Sarai. So Pharaoh summoned Abram and said, 'What is this you have done to me? Why did you not tell me she was your wife? Why did you say, "She is my sister", so that I took her for my wife? Now, here is your wife. Take her and go!' Pharaoh committed him to men who escorted him back to the frontier with his wife and all he possessed.
>
> Gen 12:10–20

Abram returned to the place where he had built his altar. To avoid a dispute with his nephew, Lot, over pasture lands for their herds, Abram proposed that they part company. Lot was a rather weak and pleasure-loving man, but Abram always dealt kindly with him, letting him have the first choice of land, and later rescuing him from some enemies.

Lot chose the Jordan Valley. God then renewed His promise, giving Canaan to Abram and his descendants. This promise by God to Abram became a central theme in the history of the Hebrews, Abram's descendants, and was transformed to have universal meaning by Jesus. Jesus invited all men, all men and women of all times, to enter the heavenly promised land, called God's kingdom.

During all his years of wandering, Abram, imperfect as he was, had been faithful to God's commands. But he was puzzled. Just what was the meaning of repeated promises about his descendants when he had no children at all? Finally he asked God the question that was bothering him. Remember that "Yahweh" is the word for God:

> 'My Lord Yahweh,' Abram replied 'what do you intend to give me? I go childless . . . ' Then Abram said, 'See, you have given me no descendants; some man of my household will be my heir'. And then this word of Yahweh was spoken to him, 'He shall not be your heir; your heir shall be of your own flesh and blood'. Then taking him outside he said, 'Look up to heaven and count the stars if you can. Such will be your descendants' he told him. Abram put his faith in Yahweh, who counted this as making him justified.
>
> Gen 15:2-6

Sarai, Abram's wife, was anxious about her childlessness. Following a custom of that time, she gave her slave Hagar to Abram so that he could have children by her. Hagar gave birth to a son, whom Abram named Ishmael. Thirteen more years passed.

God renewed His promises to Abram (which means "high father") yet another time. This time he changed Abram's name to Abraham, which is interpreted to mean "father of a multitude." Sarai's name was changed to Sarah: would her destiny now change? At this time also God told Abraham that all his male descendants were to be circumcised, or have a little piece of skin removed from their organ of reproduction, so as to have a sign of their membership in the family of God on their bodies. This sign is replaced in the Christian Church by baptism, which leaves no visible mark and is given to women as well as men.

At the promise of a son, Abraham laughed this time. Shall a man who is one hundred years old and a woman who is ninety have a son? But he and all the men in his household were immediately circumcised. He did what God told him to do.

Sarah also thought the idea that she would have a son so late in life was laughable. God questioned them both about this doubt, and reminded them that nothing was too wonderful for God to do. When Sarah does have a son she reinterprets her laughter, saying,

"God has given me cause to laugh" (Gen 21:6). Her son was named "Isaac" which means "God has smiled".

Paul often spoke of Isaac's birth as due to the faith of Abraham and Sarah. In one of his letters Paul says that because of this faith, there came from a man already as good as dead himself, as many descendants as the stars of heaven. Jesus spoke of the necessity of rebirth through faith, an idea foreshadowed in Abraham. In a moment we will come to a final story showing that the descendants of Abraham have a special destiny anchored in the faith that what God promises, He will fulfill, if men respond to His demands with perfect confidence in Him.

Abraham had very realistic conversations with God. God told him that He was planning to destroy Sodom because the people there were so wicked. But Abraham said, what if there are fifty just men in Sodom? Surely you are not going to treat the just and the wicked in the same way? God replied that if He found fifty just men in the town, He would spare the whole place because of them. But, Abraham said, what if the number of the just is only 45, or 40, or 30, or only 10? God said that He would spare Sodom for the sake of 10 just men, as later in the parable of the weeds and the wheat Jesus said that the weeds should be left so as not to root up the good wheat. This explains why the wicked are not punished immediately. Unfortunately, God's three investigating angels did not find even ten just men, and Sodom was destroyed.

Now that Sarah had a son she asked Abraham to send Hagar and Ishmael away. Abraham was upset. Was not Ishmael his son? But God told Abraham to do as Sarah wished, for Isaac was the son of the promise. Paul speaks of Isaac as having been born in the Spirit's way, as compared with the ordinary way in which Ishmael was born.

But Abraham must undergo one more test of his faith, and final confirmation of the promise.

It happened some time later that God put Abraham to the test. 'Abraham, Abraham' he called. 'Here I am' he replied. 'Take your son,' God said 'your only child Isaac, whom you love, and go to the land of Moriah. There you shall offer him as a burnt offering, on a mountain I will point out to you.'

Rising early next morning Abraham saddled his ass and took

with him two of his servants and his son Isaac. He chopped
wood for the burnt offering and started on his journey to the
place God had pointed out to him. On the third day Abraham
looked up and saw the place in the distance. Then Abraham
said to his servants, 'Stay here with the donkey. The boy and
I will go over there; we will worship and come back to you.'

Abraham took the wood for the burnt offering, loaded it
on Isaac, and carried in his own hands the fire and the knife.
Then the two of them set out together. Isaac spoke to his father
Abraham, 'Father,' he said. 'Yes, my son' he replied. 'Look,'
he said 'here are the fire and the wood, but where is the lamb
for the burnt offering?' Abraham answered, 'My son, God
himself will provide the lamb for the burnt offering'. Then
the two of them went on together.

When they arrived at the place God had pointed out to him,
Abraham built an altar there, and arranged the wood. Then
he bound his son Isaac and put him on the altar on top of
the wood. Abraham stretched out his hand and seized the
knife to kill his son.

But the angel of Yahweh called to him from heaven. 'Abraham, Abraham' he said. 'I am here' he replied. Do not raise
your hand against the boy' the angel said. 'Do not harm him,
for now I know you fear God. You have not refused me your
son, your only son.' Then looking up, Abraham saw a ram
caught by its horns in a bush. Abraham took the ram and
offered it as a burnt-offering in place of his son. . . .

The angel of Yahweh called Abraham a second time from
heaven. 'I swear by my own self — it is Yahweh who speaks —
because you have done this, because you have not refused me
your son, I will shower blessings on you, I will make your
descendants as many as the stars of heaven and the grains
of sand on the seashore. Your descendants shall gain possession
of the gates of their enemies. All the nations of the earth shall
bless themselves by your descendants, as a reward for your
obedience.'

Gen 22:2–18

6. Descendants of the Promise

Sarah died. Abraham was no longer a youth so anxious for life as to lose confidence in God, but an old man anticipating God's desires so that he might die. What more might Abraham do for God? Can you guess? This is what he did.

He called the eldest servant of his household. He had a special mission for him to carry out. If the promise is to be fulfilled, Abraham's son Isaac must have children, and, of course, a wife to be the mother of these children. She must not be a Canaanite woman, but a woman from the kin of Abraham. Later in history a number of alien and sinful women entered into the lineage which terminated in Jesus, but by their time the family had evolved into a race and the message had a context of law and an accumulated history to support it. Abraham was the custodian of the fragile seed. He did not think that his son, Isaac, should return to the home which God had told him to leave. Instead, a servant is to go there to find and bring back the wife God has set apart for Isaac.

This servant set out with a caravan of ten camels. He was given a sign by which to identify the chosen girl: she would be hospitable. When asked for a drink of water she would not only offer it, but offer to water the camels too. This Rebekah did. She ran back and forth, filling her pitcher at a spring and emptying it in a trough the animals could drink from. And ten camels can drink a lot of water! How did the servant react when he saw the sign fulfilled? He weighted Rebekah down, literally, with bracelets and put a ring through her nose!

On enquiry, the servant found Rebekah to be a relative of Abraham's. He explained his mission to her family, who said they could not refuse what God commanded. The caravan returned to

Palestine with Rebekah. When Rebekah saw Isaac, even before she knew who he was, she was attracted to him. He, in turn, loved her profoundly. Old Abraham died, having wandered for many years since he had first been sent forth by God.

The children of Rebekah and Isaac

After a long period of barrenness Rebekah had twin sons. Notice that the mothers of the chosen sons are without children until God sends them, emphasizing that they are His gift. The lives of the twins, Esau and Jacob, illustrate the theme of God's choice once again. All these stories show that it does not matter who the actors are; God's will is carried out. God uses events as He sees fit. He can choose to prefer the younger son, even though society considers the older son the rightful heir.

Esau was the elder son. He showed that he valued his rights as the first born of the twins so little that he voluntarily exchanged them with Jacob for a bowl of lentil soup! Later, when it came time for Isaac to die, Jacob tricked his father into giving him the blessing intended for the first born.

The old patriarch was blind. Jacob put the skins of lambs on his arms so that he would be hairy to touch as his brother Esau was. Rebekah dressed him in Esau's clothes. He lied to his father, telling him that he was Esau.

Isaac gave Jacob the blessing which carried God's promise. The whole affair seems to us to be very mean and deceitful. But God had predestined Jacob to be the son of the promise, and Esau had abandoned his claims with the lentil soup incident. Paul condemned Esau as one who degraded religion by selling his birthright for a single meal.

The story of Jacob, which again tells us that God directs human destinies, is a great love story as was the story of Abraham. Abraham's love for Sarah was shown to be very different from his relationship with Hagar. He was characteristically kind to Hagar, but he loved Sarah profoundly.

Don't you think it is significant that God's choice of a people and each man's choice of a particular woman are put together in the Bible? Each of the chosen women was (so the biblical writers tell us) especially beautiful, but otherwise they were quite ordinary.

[25]

They were thoroughly nasty when they wanted to be. They were not perfect in our sense of the word. Far from it. But their husband's love for them never wavered. Neither did their love for their husbands.

Doesn't this suggest an answer to the questions we ask about God's choices? We know from experience, or will someday, the arbitrary seeming choice of love between one man and one woman. How deep and faithful it *can* be! How devoid of perfection each partner can be! We are all sinners: what is important is trust in God. This trust is the perfection God seeks. We can understand God's choice of His people as being like love. Let us see how God's promises are put together in the story of Jacob.

Jacob set out to find a wife among Rebekah's relatives. He went in obedience to his parent's wishes, but he seems to have been rather afraid to go on such a long journey. When the first night came he lay down to sleep using a stone for a pillow, and he had a dream. In this dream he saw a ladder reaching from earth to heaven. The angels of God were going up it and coming down, and God was there. God told Jacob that He was protecting him wherever he might be. When Jacob woke up he said, "God is in this place and I never knew it." Jacob had not yet understood what his grandfather Abraham knew so well: that God is everywhere, next to us no matter where we are, protecting His chosen friends.

So Jacob continued his journey toward the east until he came to a well that was blocked by a heavy stone. His cousin Rachel, who was a shepherdess, came there to water her sheep. Jacob was so excited to have found the family of his mother Rebekah — or, perhaps, it was love at first sight — that he rolled back the enormous stone, kissed Rachel and burst into tears! His uncle Laban came running and they kissed each other also. They didn't kiss when they parted twenty years later — you will see.

Because Jacob had fallen in love with Rachel, he agreed to work for his uncle Laban for seven years in order to marry her. The seven years seemed to him like a few days, he loved her so much. After seven years he asked that they be married.

Laban held a big wedding feast. When the first night came he substituted his unattractive older daughter, Leah, for Rachel, the younger daughter. This was easy to do since the bride was covered and veiled according to the customs of the time.

In the morning, finding that Leah had been substituted for Rachel, Jacob was angry. Laban excused himself, saying that according to the local custom the younger daughter could not marry before the older one, but Jacob could marry Rachel the next week in return for seven more years of work. Jacob agreed. He married Rachel and worked seven more years for Laban, and then more years for livestock of his own.

The Bible gives a graphic picture of the big family of Jacob. Leah and Rachel each had a slave girl. Jacob had children by all four women: his two wives and their slave girls. His wives offered their slaves to him when they appeared unable to bear children. Leah had six or seven children before Joseph was born to Rachel. Benjamin was born last. In all Jacob had twelve sons, and at least one daughter. But it was the sons who were important. They became the founders of the twelve tribes into which the Israelite people were organized. The number twelve became extremely significant. Jesus founded the Church on twelve men, His apostles. The heavenly Jerusalem had twelve gates in John's great visions, and so on.

After twenty years had passed Jacob decided to return to his home. He and his uncle Laban had a battle of wits over ownership of the livestock. Each deceived the other. Finally, Jacob outwitted Laban and fled. He put his children and wives on camels and drove the livestock before him. Such migrations over the semi-desert land must have been exciting, hard work, and dangerous. Rachel stole her father's idols in the get-away.

Laban pursued Jacob. He especially wanted his household idols. Jacob, not knowing that Rachel had stolen them, gave Laban permission to search his encampment. Rachel sat on the idols to hide them and Laban did not find them. Thinking Laban had made a false accusation, Jacob lost his temper and listed all the ways his father-in-law had exploited him. You ought to read this almost Shakespearean speech. It can be found in Genesis 31:36 to 42. Jacob wound up by saying that if God had not protected him, Laban would have sent him away empty-handed after all his work for the older man.

But Laban, who had been warned by God to say nothing to

Jacob, gave a fair and cool reply. He observed that the wives and vast possessions Jacob now had, had all once belonged to him. So the two men settled on a boundary between them.

But now Jacob had to face his brother Esau. He was afraid, for he heard that Esau was coming with 400 men. What did Jacob do? He set aside droves of goats, sheep, camels, cows and donkeys as gifts for Esau, and had a servant drive each group of animals. He had the groups spaced out, so Esau would receive each separately. Don't you think Jacob was a shrewd psychologist? Jacob sent his family and the rest of his possessions across a river and stayed alone.

Jacob becomes Israel

That night Jacob encountered God in a strange way:

> And there was one that wrestled with him until daybreak who, seeing that he could not master him, struck him in the socket of his hip, and Jacob's hip was dislocated as he wrestled with him. He said, 'Let me go, for day is breaking'. But Jacob answered, 'I will not let you go unless you bless me'. He then asked, 'What is your name?' 'Jacob', he replied. He said, 'Your name shall no longer be Jacob, but Israel, because you have been strong against God, you shall prevail against men'. Jacob then made this request, 'I beg you, tell me your name', but he replied, 'Why do you ask my name?' And he blessed him there.
>
> Jacob named the place Peniel, 'Because I have seen God face to face,' he said 'and I have survived'.
>
> Gen 32:26–31

After all that preparation and such a string of lavish gifts, Esau gave Jacob a big welcome. Esau took Jacob in his arms and wept. He invited Jacob to his camp. Jacob did not go with him, however. In the long run two such nomad leaders could not live near one another for they had more livestock than the land could support. Jacob moved south gradually.

At Bethlehem, the place where Jesus was born, Rachel died giving birth to the last of Israel's twelve sons. With her last breath Rachel named him Ben-oni which means "son of my sorrow," but Israel changed the name to Benjamin, or "son of happy omen." Israel always loved Joseph and Benjamin, the two children of his beloved Rachel, more than any of his other sons.

7. The Sale of the Promised Son

With the story of Joseph we meet modern social questions for the first time in the Bible although the biblical writer was neither interested in, nor passing judgment on, these things which we are aware of. See if you agree that Joseph faced problems we face today when you have finished reading this chapter.

Of course, Joseph's story is also a revelation: it shows how God uses the actions of men to serve His own purposes. These two ideas do not conflict. But let us see, together, how love, jealousy and deceit, natural disaster, the interpretation of dreams and administrative ability all fit together to further God's plans for mankind.

Israel had twelve sons. Joseph was second youngest and Benjamin was the very last. These two were the children of Rachel, whom you remember, was Jacob's beloved. The Bible says that Israel loved Joseph more than all his other sons. But his brothers hated him for being their father's favorite.

Joseph, himself, made matters worse with his brothers because of his dreams. In one dream he and his brothers were binding wheat into sheaves, that is, bundles of the stalks (not bales such as we make with machines). Joseph saw his sheaf rise up. All the other sheaves bowed to his. When Joseph told this dream to his brothers they said, "so you want to lord it over us." But the dream was a true prophecy of what happened later.

In another dream he saw the sun and the moon and eleven stars bowing to him. What do you think this dream meant? It was clear to his family. Even his father was angry and scolded him about this dream. But it was not a projection of his own ambitions; it was a preview of God's plan.

When Joseph was seventeen his father sent him on an errand to his brothers, who were pasturing their sheep. He was still far away when the brothers saw him approaching. They plotted to put him to death, but Reuben deterred them, saying, "throw him into this dry well in the wilderness instead." Reuben wanted to save his life.

So when Joseph arrived they grabbed him and tore off the coat with long sleeves his father had given him. He cried for mercy but they made fun of him and threw him into a dry well. They covered the coat with blood from a goat and sent it home, saying, "look what we found in the wilderness." Israel thought a wild beast must have killed Joseph, and mourned a very long time for the boy.

Joseph is sold by his brothers

How did Joseph get out of the well? His brother Judah persuaded the others to sell him to some merchants who passed by. The brothers pulled him out and sold him for twenty pieces of silver. He was taken to Egypt by a merchant caravan where he was sold again: to Potiphar, who was an official of the Pharaoh who ruled Egypt. At that time (about 1700 B.C.), Egypt was a great civilization and the valley around its river, the Nile, was densely populated. Egypt was already old and rich in art and other aspects of culture. By comparison Israel's family were rustics from a barren desert country. Their human achievements appeared insignificant. Their only wealth was their understanding of God, and the fact that God had chosen them to bring light to all mankind.

God was Joseph's protector. Everything Joseph did turned out so well that his master gave up working. He let Joseph run everything and thus gave him administrative experience. Naturally an official who did nothing but eat neglected and bored his wife. She turned from him to chase the handsome young Joseph and tried to lead Joseph into sin with her. But Joseph did not give in. He told her, with a realistic estimate of the situation, that she was the only thing her husband had not given him. He would not sin against God by making love to her. Then the frustrated woman accused Joseph of what he had not done and he was jailed for some years. For the second time Joseph was the victim of human malice. But God used his misfortune.

In jail Joseph interpreted the dreams of other prisoners. When

Pharaoh had two dreams that no one could interpret, a member of his household remembered the Hebrew interpreter of dreams who was in jail. Joseph was called to interpret the Pharaoh's dreams.

In one, seven fat cows came up out of the Nile. Then seven emaciated cows came up and ate the fat cows. In the other dream a corn stalk produced seven ears of corn which ripened beautifully, but these were followed by seven that withered. Joseph said:

'It is as I have told Pharaoh: God has revealed to Pharaoh what he is going to do. Seven years are coming, bringing great plenty to the whole land of Egypt, but seven years of famine will follow them, when all the plenty in the land of Egypt will be forgotten, and famine will exhaust the land. The famine that is to follow will be so very severe that no one will remember what plenty the country enjoyed. The reason why the dream came to Pharaoh twice is because the event is already determined by God, and God is impatient to bring it about.

'Pharaoh should now choose a man who is intelligent and wise to govern the land of Egypt. Pharaoh should take action and appoint supervisors over the land, and impose a tax of one-fifth on the land of Egypt during the seven years of plenty. They will collect all food produced during these good years that are coming. They will store the corn in Pharaoh's name, and place the food in the towns and hold it there. This food will serve as a reserve for the land during the seven years of famine that will afflict the land of Egypt. And so the land will not be destroyed by the famine.'

How do you think the Pharaoh reacted?

Pharaoh and all his ministers approved of what he had said. Then Pharaoh asked his ministers, 'Can we find any other man like this, possessing the spirit of God?' So Pharaoh said to Joseph, 'Seeing that God has given you knowledge of all this, there can be no one as intelligent and wise as you. You shall be my chancellor, and all my people shall respect your orders; only this throne shall set me above you.' Pharaoh said to Joseph, 'I hereby make you governor of the whole land of Egypt'. Pharaoh took the ring from his hand and put it on Joseph's. He clothed him in fine linen and put a gold chain round his neck. He made him ride in the best chariot he had after his

[31]

own, and they cried before him 'Abrek'. This is the way he was made governor of the whole land of Egypt.

Gen 41:28–43

The Pharaoh was impressed by Joseph's interpretations of his dreams. He recognized that God had given Joseph this knowledge. No man in Egypt could match his wisdom. So he appointed Joseph to rule Egypt next after himself, and gave him a wife from the Egyptian aristocracy. Joseph put his plan to prepare for the famine into operation. During the seven fruitful years an immense amount of grain was stored in all the towns of Egypt.

Then the years of famine came. Joseph began to sell the grain he had stored. Soon the terrible drought brought starvation not only to Egypt, but to all the surrounding lands. Joseph's father and brothers in Canaan were starving. They heard that there was grain for sale in Egypt, so Israel sent ten of his sons to buy grain there, keeping Benjamin alone at home.

Joseph meets his brothers

When Joseph's brothers came, he recognized them, but they did not recognize him. He accused them of being spies and arrested them. He seems to have treated them as he did in order that his dreams of long ago might be fulfilled. Keeping one in prison, he sent the rest back to get Benjamin. By secretly giving their purchase money back, putting it in their bags of corn, he thoroughly frightened them.

Israel was tormented. He did not want to send Benjamin because he loved him so. Famine forced him to comply. The brother's caravan returned to Egypt, rich with gifts, and with Benjamin.

When Joseph saw them he invited them to a feast at his house. They were more afraid than ever and bowed before Joseph. But later when he sent them away he again returned their money and also had a silver cup put in Benjamin's sack. This time he sent men to pursue them and accuse them of stealing the silver cup. They pleaded passionately for their lives before Joseph. When Judah told Joseph how his father Israel was tormented because of his love for Benjamin, Joseph broke down and revealed to them who he was. Throwing his arms around Benjamin he wept. He kissed all his brothers. Joseph had Israel and all his people brought to a rich part

[32]

of Egypt called Goshen, where they settled.

Meanwhile Joseph exploited the advantages his economic planning had given him. When the people had no more money to buy grain, he accepted their lands. He made Egypt a completely socialist state in which Pharaoh owned all the lands and the people were his serfs.

Throughout history Joseph has been the symbol of the provider of the people. He did provide for the people in a time of severe famine. But how? Joseph himself neither grew nor harvested the wheat he sold — and sold at the stiff price of the people's freedom. It is misleading to speak of him as caring for the household of Pharaoh as if his work were domestic and immediate. As the chief administrator of a nation having perhaps between ten and thirteen million people, he was a sophisticated, urbane, modern type social planner and power politician.

Centuries later the Hebrews found themselves suffering from slavery to the Pharaoh. This too was in keeping with God's plan. God had told Abraham that, though his descendants would inherit the promised land, before this happened they would be exiled and enslaved for four hundred years. This exile began with Joseph.

The first Christian martyr, Stephen, made a speech about the works of God before he was stoned to death. This is how he summed up the history of Joseph in his speech:

> The actual words God used when he spoke to him [Abraham] that *his descendants would be exiles in a foreign land, where they would be slaves and oppressed for four hundred years.* *"But I will pass judgement on the nation that enslaves them"* God said *"and after this they will leave, and worship me in this place."* Then he made the covenant of circumcision: so when his son Isaac was born he circumcised him on the eighth day. Isaac did the same for Jacob, and Jacob for the twelve patriarchs.
>
> 'The patriarchs were *jealous of Joseph and sold him into slavery in Egypt.* But *God was with him,* and rescued him from all his miseries by making him wise enough to attract the attention of Pharaoh king of Egypt, who *made him governor of Egypt* and put him in charge of the royal household. *Then a famine came* that caused much suffering *throughout Egypt and Canaan,* and our ancestors could find nothing to eat. When

Jacob *heard that there was grain for sale in Egypt,* he sent our ancestors there on a first visit, but it was on the second that *Joseph made himself known to his brothers,* and told Pharaoh about his family. Joseph then sent for his father Jacob and his whole family, a total of *seventy-five people.'*

Acts 7:9–14

8. Tell My People To Go

Have you noticed that God's chosen people were nomadic herds-
men, not farmers or city dwellers? The study of the many, many
religions in which men have believed shows that people living these
different forms of life tend to seek God differently. Nomadic groups
have their tribal god, while farmers have many nature gods. Urban
people are tempted to deify their kings.

Farmers are anxious about human and agricultural fertility; their
gods support (or blight) the fruitfulness of the land, personifying
the forces of nature. The farmers' world has a cyclic rhythm of
growth, decline and then the miraculous seeming rebirth of all
living things after winter, or the dry season. Is it surprising that
many farming cultures have believed in the endless transmigra-
tion of souls and thought of life as a repetition rather than a "going
somewhere"?

By comparison the herdsman is in a circumstance of group unity,
mobility, continuous growth, division, and dispersal. You saw how
the herds of Laban and Jacob, and also their families, steadily increased. Abraham and Lot, Laban and Jacob, Jacob and Esau:
these pairs of tribal leaders separated when the growth of their
herds became too great for the land to support. Free and mobile,
with well defined ideas of private property, they moved on to seek
new pastures. They carried their ideas abroad with them.

The life of cities requires more complex human organization than
does herding or farming. The leader must have ministers of this and
that and the people become specialists providing services for each
other. No one is autonomous with his family and herds, nor self-
sufficient on the land so long as the forces of nature remain orderly.
Instead men depend on the human order and the strength of the

regulator of that order. God tends to become identified with the king who regulates the urban structure of inter-dependencies. Worship tends to become a link in the social system.

When the Hebrews became farmers and city-dwellers they did not lose their belief in Yahweh, the one God directing continuous growth and development, independent of nature, who had singled them out to lead all mankind toward a new future. The Hebrews were very, very tempted by the nature and fertility gods their neighbors worshipped. They were tempted to reject Yahweh for a king. Many among them gave in to these temptations, but not the entire people. Even when their kings turned to the worship of idols the country people, the poor in particular, remained faithful to Yahweh. Dispersed and scattered over the ancient middle east (or perhaps aided by these misfortunes) a Hebrew remnant held on to the spiritual wisdom of their ancestors. God preserved a portion of His people as His witnesses, always tutoring them through the events of history as interpreted by His prophets and the authors of scripture.

Ultimately the savior, Jesus Christ, was born among the faithful remnant of the worshippers of Yahweh. Jesus explicitly commanded His followers to extend faith in God to all mankind. He brought God's teaching to a climax in Himself and led mankind into the new spiritual kingdom, prefigured in the promises made to the Hebrews. Before Jesus a people grew in readiness to receive the savior; after Jesus growth became a "putting on of Christ."

But before the long centuries of evolution from nomadic to agricultural and to urban life, from limited promise to universal mission, from the covenant of the law to that of the Spirit, the Hebrews were unified in the desert void. Homeless in the inhospitable desert wastelands they were truly an empty handed and impotent people. It was through the exodus that God unified His chosen people. It was in the desert that they reached adulthood as a people. There God revealed His will through Moses.

The youth of Moses

The scene of God's action is in Egypt as Exodus, the second book of the Bible, opens. The Hebrews are slaves of the Pharaoh. They are in exile from the promised land. And they are suffering.

But the number of Abraham's descendants has increased so much that the Egyptians are alarmed.

Pharaoh then gave this command: throw all the boys born to the Hebrews into the river, but let all the girls live. Now a beautiful boy was born to a couple of the tribe of Levi. The boy's mother kept him hidden for three months and then, when she could hide him no longer, devised this scheme to save his life.

Do you already know what she did? She found a basket and made it waterproof. Then she put the baby in the basket and left it among the reeds by the water's edge, near the spot where Pharaoh's daughter went to bathe. When the Pharaoh's daughter saw the baby she knew it was a Hebrew boy, and was sorry for the baby who was crying. Now Moses' older sister was watching. She ran up and asked Pharaoh's daughter if she could find a nurse to care for the baby for her. The Egyptian princess said yes. Of course, Moses' sister found their mother. So Pharaoh's daughter paid Moses' own mother to bring the baby up, and when he grew up Pharaoh's daughter adopted him as her son.

But Moses knew he was a Hebrew. One day when he saw an Egyptian beating a Hebrew he got angry and killed the Egyptian. Because of this he fled from Egypt to the land of Midian where he settled with a priest named Jethro. He married one of Jethro's daughters and stayed there a long time. In Egypt Hebrew slaves were crying out to God for help.

God calls Moses to his vocation

One day Moses was caring for Jethro's sheep. He took the flock to the far side of the wilderness, to Horeb or Sinai, the mountain of God. God appeared to him there in the form of a flame coming from the middle of a bush. At first, Moses was astonished because the bush was blazing but it was not being burnt up. He went to look closer. God called to him "Moses, Moses," but told him not to go nearer. God said to Moses:

'. . . the cry of the sons of Israel has come to me, and I have witnessed the way in which the Egyptians oppress them, so come, I send you to Pharaoh to bring the sons of Israel, my people, out of Egypt.'

Ex 3:9–10

[37]

Moses had a few doubts about himself. He said to God, "who am I?" and "how can I do such a thing?" But God said He would be with Moses. Then Moses said:

'I am to go, then, to the sons of Israel and say to them, "The God of your fathers has sent me to you". But if they ask me what his name is, what am I to tell them?' And God said to Moses, 'I Am who I AM. This' he said 'is what you must say to the sons of Israel: "I Am has sent me to you".' And God also said to Moses, 'You are to say to the sons of Israel: "Yahweh, the God of your fathers, the God of Abraham, the God of Isaac, and the God of Jacob, has sent me to you". This is my name for all time; by this name I shall be invoked for all generations to come."

Ex 3:13–15

God instructed Moses first to gather the Hebrews in support of His plan to bring them out of Egypt, and then to ask permission of Pharaoh for the whole people to make a journey into the wilderness to offer sacrifice. God said that Pharaoh would refuse until he was forced. Moses still protested that no one would listen to him, so God gave him magic tricks to impress them. When Moses threw his staff, or walking stick, on the ground it became a snake, but when he caught the snake by the tail it became a staff again. God gave Moses a number of tricks of this sort.

Moses found that the Egyptian sorcerers could match his magic tricks. Stronger measures were needed. So God inflicted ten plagues on the Egyptians by the hands of Moses: He turned their rivers into blood, and caused the country to be overrun by frogs, then by mosquitos and gladflies. Then He killed the Egyptian's livestock and caused the people to suffer from boils. He sent hail and locusts. Three days of darkness covered Egypt as the ninth plague. Still Pharaoh would not give in.

The Passover and flight

Now God told the Hebrews to prepare themselves so as to be spared the tenth plague. As a preparation for this final plague and their flight He gave special meaning to the passover supper. God explained how each family was to gather and eat together a roast lamb. They were to eat it with unleavened bread and bitter herbs, and not to break any of its bones or leave any left-overs. The people were to wear clothes suitable for a journey and eat in haste. A little of the lamb's blood was to be smeared around the doors of the Hebrew's houses so that the angels of the tenth plague might recognize and spare them. This is the way the event was re-enacted at the time the story of Moses was written down.

In the New Testament the Passover lamb is identified with Jesus. His sacrifice is for all mankind. Jesus' followers are marked by His saving blood, which they receive in communion. When the soldiers refrained from breaking Jesus' bones because He was already dead on the cross they unwittingly fulfilled prophecies, as John notes. Like the Passover lamb, his bones were not broken.

The night of the first Passover God killed all the first born in Egypt, from the Pharaoh's own heir to the prisoner in the dungeon. No Egyptian house was spared its death while the Hebrews fled from the Nile valley.

The Bible says that the Israelites, or Hebrews, with other people who joined them, numbered 600,000 men (a symbolic number) not counting their families. Their exile in Egypt had lasted over 400 years, as God had predicted to Abraham. The Israelites fled by a round-about way, pursued by all the chariots, horsemen, and army of Egypt. Don't imagine the chariots you have seen on movie race courses — this was a long trip, and not on any super highway. When the Hebrews saw this army pursuing them the people were frightened and complained to Moses, "Were there no graves in Egypt that you must lead us out to die in the wilderness?" Moses told them to have no fear. And God said, march on.

The angel of God who went before them in the pillar of cloud changed his position to the rear. The enemy got no closer that night. In the morning Moses stretched out his hand over the sea. God had driven the sea back with a strong wind all night. The waters parted and the sons of Israel crossed on dry land.

The Egyptians gave chase into the sea bed. Their chariot wheels clogged and they became confused and panicked. God told Moses to stretch out his hand again. The waters returned; all the Egyptians were drowned. The Israelites then joyfully worshipped God. They had a great celebration and composed a long song about what had happened. Here is a small part of their song:

[39]

"This is my God, I praise him;
the God of my father, I extol him.
Yahweh is a warrior;
Yahweh is his name.
The chariots and the army of Pharaoh he has hurled into the sea;
the pick of his horsemen lie drowned in the Sea of Reeds.
The depths have closed over them;
they have sunk to the bottom like a stone.
Your right hand, Yahweh, shows majestic in power,
your right hand, Yahweh, shatters the enemy."

Ex 15:2–6

But it wasn't long before the fugitives found themselves without food and began to complain. They believed in God but were quick to lose trust in Him when crises came. God fed them in the desert by sending quail in the evening and a fine substance in the morning which was something like bread. The Israelites called this substance manna. Many Christians see in this manna a foreshadowing of the Eucharist, the form in which Jesus is given to mankind as the bread of eternal life. The Hebrews lived on manna for forty years in the desert. Aaron, Moses' brother, kept a jar of it according to God's instructions, to be put later with the tablets of the law in the ark of the covenant. At one time when the people were without water Moses hit a rock with his staff and water flowed out for the people. Thus God provided for the people in the desert on a day to day basis.

9. Laws for a People Ruled by God

But what about the law? Probably you have heard that God gave the ten commandments to Moses. How did that happen? Possibly Moses went off alone up a mountain so he could be undistracted and respond to God's inspirations, and, simultaneously, there were violent storms in the mountain top. This is what we might have said about it in our "literary genre" or "style." But, in what is called the "literary genre," "style" or "mode of expression" of the biblical peoples, the account is much more dramatic. This is how the Bible tells about the origin of the Mosaic law.

The people were camped near Mount Sinai in the desert. God came down on the mountain top in a dense cloud, with thunder and lightning flashes. The people trembled at the bottom of the mountain while Moses climbed up into the cloud. There God gave Moses a civil code for His people, inscribed on two stone tablets. In Israel's law all things we call profane were permeated by the sacred. The law was not a constitution but a spelling-out of the divine-human relationship.

The ten commandments are part of the law God gave Moses. They are called the "Decalogue," and first appear in chapter twenty of the Book of Exodus, and again in the fifth chapter of Deuteronomy. Jesus repeated and summarized them:

> Jesus said, 'You must love the Lord your God with all your heart, with all your soul, and with all your mind. This is the greatest and the first commandment. The second resembles it: you must love your neighbor as yourself. On these two commandments hang the whole Law, and the Prophets also.'
>
> Mt 22:37–40

Here are key lines from the text of the ten commandments given in the Book of Exodus. The first three commandments have to do with the love of God, which Jesus put first. The other seven show how to relate to your neighbor so that this love can break through and resemble the love of the first commandment.

'I am Yahweh your God . . . You shall have no gods except me.

You shall not make yourself a carved image . . . bow down to them or serve them . . .

You shall not utter the name of Yahweh your God to misuse it . . .

Remember the sabbath day and keep it holy . . . You shall do no work on that day . . .

Honour your father and your mother . . .

You shall not kill.

You shall not commit adultery.

You shall not steal.

You shall not bear false witness against your neighbor.

You shall not covet your neighbor's house . . . your neighbor's wife . . . or anything that is his.'

Ex 20:1–17 (selected)

Today some people ask, "Why are the commandments stated negatively instead of positively like Jesus' summary?" But it is appropriate to law to be negative so as not to limit positive action. Laws exclude freedom in what they apply to; the negative statement makes this area in which freedom is excluded as small as possible. The positive formulas given by Jesus are guides to the use of this freedom and thus express the spirit of the law. To fulfill Jesus' positive command is the creative work of a lifetime.

It is also said, nowadays, that the law cannot oblige because nothing but love is true, and love must be voluntary and free of restraint. But how can one tell which of two or three acts is the more perfect application of love? This is a difficult question. The commandments make this question easier to answer by listing some of the major ways in which men and women have from time immemorial turned away from God, injured themselves and failed to respect their neighbors. They are keys to spiritual, personal and social integrity.

Obeying the commandments alone is not sufficient for a holy life, but it is a good beginning, as is shown by the story of Jesus and the rich young man. We will come to that story in the New Testament part of this book. By Jesus' time the Hebrews, and other people also, had accumulated more moral history than at the time of the commandments so that Jesus spoke in a way that was different from Moses' way. The exodus took place sometime between 1250 and 1230 B.C. At least the ten commandments appear to be that ancient, although the other laws given in the early part of the Bible are a collection from various periods.

This time of Moses is at the end of the late bronze age. Try to imagine a time in history when almost everything you have learned and almost every great philosopher or scientist or politician, writer or artist or saint had not yet been born. Maybe you find it easy to forget everything you know? Not really! Or, you say, that's fine for then, but what about now? Well, what about now? Much good is being done today, surely. We meet many sensitive people who have been enriched with the wisdom humanity has accumulated through the help of God. But, considering all we come by so easily today, we ought to be further along the way. By now at least the ten commandments ought to "come naturally." And we all know that movie makers, politicians, lawyers, psychiatrists and a lot of other people would have to change most of their business if the ten commandments did "come naturally."

Along with the law God gave a motive for obeying it: you will live long and prosperously, and so will your children and grandchildren. As for the promised land: its cities have been built, its wells dug, its vineyards planted; you will inherit these things you did not work to produce.

Similarly, the New Testament teaches us that we will inherit a kingdom which we do not merit. This promise to God's chosen people seems almost unjust, but are we not all in the same position? Then as now, or vice versa if you prefer, the covenant between God and His people was not a legal one in a contractual or a domineering sense. It was, and is, not earned or merited. It was, and is, a gift of love to a sinful, undeserving people. This is well explained in Deuteronomy, chapters six and seven.

[43]

False worship

Moses was gone from the encampment for forty days and forty nights. It seemed a long time to the people at the foot of the mountain and they gave him up for lost. They made themselves a new god, a golden calf, and worshipped it. Aaron cast the calf and supervised the sacrifices to it. God was angry and told Moses He was going to destroy this headstrong and faithless people, but Moses pleaded for them. Then he returned to the camp with the tablets of the law.

When he saw the people singing and dancing around the golden calf, he too got angry. He threw down the tablets, breaking them. Seizing the golden idol he ground it into powder. Moses cried out, "Who is on my side?" The sons of Levi joined him. Moses sent them into the camp to kill the idolaters: they slew 3000 of the men. Thus the sons of Levi were made the priestly caste in Israel. Moses kept his leadership. The tablets were re-done and put in the Ark of the Testimony.

Moses also made a place of worship, a tabernacle or "Tent of Meeting," according to God's instructions. The Israelites moved on toward the promised land under Moses' leadership with the pillar of cloud before them by day and a pillar of fire by night.

Many of the ideas in this chapter are summed up in the short Psalm numbered 15:

The Guest of Yahweh

Psalms of David

Yahweh, who has the right to enter your tent,
or to live on your holy mountain?

The man whose way of life is blameless,
who always does what is right,
who speaks the truth from his heart,
whose tongue is not used for slander,

who does no wrong to his fellow,
casts no discredit on his neighbor,

looks with contempt on the reprobate,
but honours those who fear Yahweh;
Who stands by his pledge at any cost,
does not ask interest on loans,
and cannot be bribed to victimize the innocent.
— If a man does all this, nothing can ever shake him.

10. In Sight of Fulfillment

The Israelites had moved near to the promised land. God told Moses to send scouts to look the land over. Moses sent an important man from each tribe .After forty days they came back and gave their report. They found milk and honey to be the products of the land. But they also found the land occupied by a number of powerful peoples.

One of the scouts, Caleb, said, "We must march in and conquer this land and we can do it." Joshua agreed with Caleb but the others were afraid. They said, "We are too few to conquer this land. We will die by the sword and our wives and children will be taken as booty." The fearful men convinced the people.

Then God was angered because the Israelites had so little confidence in Him after He had saved them so often and so miraculously. He killed all the pessimistic scouts, sparing the optimists Caleb and Joshua, and told Moses to march the Hebrews back into the wilderness until the generation which had originally left Egypt was dead. Only the young children whom the pessimists had said would be seized as booty were to enter the promised land.

Moses was then faced with a revolt. The earth opened and swallowed the leaders of the revolt with their families, while a fire from heaven burned up other rebels. The revolt had overtones of a popular revolution against official authorities; God supported the official authorities in this case. Nonetheless, religion and secular life in Israel were not as dependent on human authorities as in other societies of time. God was Israel's only authority; all others were His servants. The attitudes of the whole people were important — more often a cause for God's wrath than His blessing in time of crisis. At a later period in Hebrew history it was the country people, as opposed to the leaders and city dwellers, who remained loyal to God.

Because of these rebellions the wrath of God continued with a plague against the people. Moses sent Aaron in haste to perform the rite of atonement over the people. Aaron stood with the dead to one side and the living on the other when the plague stopped. Maybe it did happen this way, or maybe he set up a quarantine. The biblical account is not a literal history, but at this distance in time we cannot analyze all the events according to our ways of interpreting them.

Another time God sent serpents to destroy the sinful people. Moses pleaded for them and God told him to make a fiery serpent and raise it on a standard. He made it of bronze. Those who looked at it were saved. All in all, the years in the desert were a troubled prelude to the stormy conquest of the promised land. Gradually groups of the impatient Israelites began their conquest of the peoples then living in Palestine.

Did you know that another "dumb" creature besides the snake in Eden said a few words recorded in the Bible? This is the story. Some enemies of Israel tried to get a pagan prophet named Balaam to curse the Israelites. He set out at their request, riding a donkey. But his donkey saw that God's angel was blocking the road and would not go on although Balaam beat her. She sat down and wouldn't move! God opened the donkey's mouth and let her scold Balaam for his cruelty. The Balaam too, saw the angel. After that Balaam could not curse the Israelites. Instead he blessed them in a series of beautiful poems, knowing that God was with them.

As the Hebrews began to get more involved with the peoples inhabiting the land, new problems arose. The Israelites were tempted to mix with them, worship their gods and intermarry. So God commanded them to destroy everyone and everything they found in Canaan. Without this command they would probably have lost their identity and their faith.

Problems also arose about the division of the land among the Israelites, Moses made practical rules about this as God instructed him to do. Here the organization into twelve tribes was important. It was a useful organizational device and such practices as the keeping of genealogies supported the social structure built on it.

Many of the "Mosaic" laws, besides keeping the organizational structure clear, also protected the people (even women and slaves) from abuses common to those times in history.

God gave Moses a vision of the promised land, which he was not himself allowed to enter. The Book of Deuteronomy ends with the praise of Moses. "Since then, never has there been such a prophet in Israel as Moses, the Man Yahweh knew face to face" (Dt 34:10).

Moses appointed Joshua as the leader of the people. Joshua held a great meeting at Shechem which pulled all the people together and united them. Although he established the chosen people in the promised land the conquest was not completed until the time of David. The city of Jerusalem, in the middle of the country, was not conquered until then.

After Joshua the Hebrews had a series of leaders called "Judges." As the Bible expresses it, God let some of the inhabitants remain on the land to test the Israelites. They failed in faith over and over again, so that the Judges constantly had to rescue them from idolatry and restore the strength which left them each time they betrayed God.

11. The First Mis-Step

God Himself ruled Israel. The relationship of His people to His sovereignty was expressed in the law of Moses. With God as their ruler and teacher this people needed no king, no other gods, and no formal constitution.

Yet after the long struggle for the promised land and the trials they had brought on themselves by their infidelities, the Israelites looked about them and saw that other nations had kings. Then they, too, wanted a king. So they spoke to the priest Samuel about their new desire. And Samuel told God. What do you think God said?

God answered Samuel, "It is me they have rejected. Let them have a king but you must warn them about the rights of kings." Samuel told the people what a bad choice they were making. How do you think kings behaved in those days? They were not symbolic figureheads ceremoniously presiding over constitutional governments like the majority of the few kings (or queens) who still reign today. This is what Samuel told the people about the rights of kings:

All that Yahweh had said Samuel repeated to the people who were asking him for a king. He said, 'These will be the rights of the king who is to reign over you. He will take your sons and assign them to his chariotry and cavalry, and they will run in front of his chariot. He will use them as leaders of a thousand and leaders of fifty; he will make them plough his ploughland and harvest his harvest and make his weapons of war and the gear for his chariots. He will also take your daughters as perfumers, cooks and bakers. He will take the best of your fields, of your vineyards and olive groves and give them to his officials. He will tithe your crops and vineyards to

provide for his eunuchs and his officials. He will take the best
of your manservants and maidservants, of your cattle and your
donkeys, and make them work for him. He will tithe your
flocks, and you yourselves will become his slaves. When that
day comes, you will cry out on account of the king you have
chosen for yourselves, but on that day God will not answer you.'

1 Sam 8:10–18

Saul is made king

At that time a good looking giant of a man named Saul was
wandering around the countryside looking for some lost donkeys,
when he came to the place where Samuel was. God had revealed
to Samuel that this Saul was to be the king the people wanted. So
Samuel met Saul at the town gate. Samuel told him that the
donkeys had been found and furthermore that he, Saul, had been
chosen by God. Samuel kissed Saul and put oil on his head, anoint-
ing him king of Israel.

Saul was given the spirit of prophecy as Samuel had predicted.
But he did not tell anyone he had been anointed king. Instead
Samuel called the people together, organized by tribes. They cast
lots by tribes and families until the king was identified: Saul was
chosen king. When the people saw him, standing head and shoulders
taller than any of them, they cried, "Long live the king."

Soon Saul consolidated his rule by a victory over some enemies.
But then he became impatient and fearful. He did not trust God.
Failure to trust in God is the basic sin from the biblical viewpoint.
Therefore, as Samuel told Saul, his rule would not last. But he did
fight, with God's help, against the Philistines all of his life, even
though it is recorded in the Bible that God regretted having made
Saul king.

God sent Samuel to find the new king he had chosen to follow
Saul; he found David, still a boy, and anointed him king. Meanwhile Saul became very moody. Saul's servants suggested that he
find a skilled harpist to soothe his spirit with music. Since David was
a talented musician he was brought to the court. Saul liked David
so much (at first) that he made him his armor-bearer, and David
and Saul's son, Jonathan, became inseparable friends. David is described as having had a pleasant personality, something not said

about many biblical leaders. His skill in music was not his only gift. He was also very strong and even killed a lion with his bare hands. As an administrator he may have been less capable, in himself, but he had a gift more important in a ruler than always making the right decisions: he surrounded himself with capable assistants, enabled them to act, took their advice, and retained their undivided loyalty most of his life. This gift became important later; at this point in his story he is still a shepherd boy.

David kills Goliath

Now it happened that at one time while Saul was king, the Philistine and the Israelite armies were drawn up face to face for battle. A Philistine giant named Goliath stepped into the space between. He wore heavy armor all over his body and carried an immense spear. Goliath challenged the Israelites to send a man to fight him alone and thus decide which army would win.

David was at his father's home in Bethlehem, but some of his older brothers were in Saul's army. David's father sent him to them with some food. He ran to the battle line. David, seeing Goliath's challenge as an insult to God, volunteered to fight against the giant.

Saul put all his own armor on David, but David found he couldn't even walk with it on. So he took it off and went up to meet Goliath in his regular clothes. He had a sling and five smooth stones in his shepherd's pouch.

Goliath cursed David. But the lad ran toward him, and taking a stone, he slung it. The stone penetrated Goliath's forehead, and the giant fell down in a coma. David had no sword so he took the sword of Goliath and with it he cut off his head. Then the Philistine army turned and fled. The Israelites pursued and defeated them.

The biblical stories, which put different earlier oral and written accounts together in one composition, are inconsistent about when Saul and David met. One account makes this the occasion. In any case, David came to be in Saul's court. The Israelites were overjoyed by their victory and composed a song, singing: "Saul has killed his thousands and David his tens of thousands." Actually David had killed only one man, but this led to the death of many enemies.

Saul, quite naturally, did not like the song. Gradually he became insanely jealous of David. Twice when David was playing the harp for him, Saul picked up a spear and threw it at him to pin him to the wall, but David ducked. Saul became afraid of David and tried many times to kill him. David must have had cool nerves; imagine playing a harp for someone who throws spears at you!

David hides from Saul

By now you must have discovered that the Bible has stories about every aspect of human life. It has stories of love and hate, strength, faithfulness and jealousy. The record of David's relationship with Jonathan is one of its greatest expressions of friendship. Jonathan and David conspired together to find out for certain what Saul thought about David. Jonathan found out: there was no doubt about it, Saul was determined to kill David. So David became a fugitive, moving constantly and hiding in various places. Saul pursued him. Once Saul was so close that David cut off a piece of his cloak, yet he spared Saul's life although he could have killed him. The details of the struggle between Saul and David are facinating to read. You can find them in the first book of Samuel, from the eighteenth chapter to the end of the book.

So many of the events in the lives of Saul and David are so vivid, that it is hard to pick just a few to retell. Since little has been said about the meaning of death since the sin of Adam I am choosing the curious story about the witch Saul consulted.

At the time this happened, Samuel, the priest, was dead. Saul was face to face with an enormous army of Philistines. He trembled; he was very afraid. Saul called on God, but God would not answer him. So he decided to consult a witch, a sort of spiritualist or medium. He went at night to this woman and asked her what she saw. She conjured up the dead Samuel.

Samuel said, "Why consult me, when God has abandoned you and turned to David. You did not obey God. This is why God treats you like this now." Then Samuel told Saul that he, Saul, would die on the morrow and that the Israelites would be defeated. What Samuel said would happen did happen.

David could have killed Saul several times. But he didn't because of his respect for the fact that God had once anointed Saul. It was the Philistines who killed Saul indirectly. They wounded him. He then killed himself according to one version, or had an alien kill him according to another. His son Jonathan died in the same battle. David mourned greatly for both of them. He composed a lament. Here is part of David's song of sorrow:

> "Saul and Jonathan, loved and lovely,
> neither in life, nor in death, were divided.
> Swifter than eagles were they,
> stronger were they than lions.
>
> O daughters of Israel, weep for Saul
> who clothed you in scarlet and fine linen,
> who set brooches of gold
> on your garments.
>
> How did the heroes fall
> in the thick of the battle?
>
> O Jonathan, in your death I am stricken,
> I am desolate for you, Jonathan my brother.
> Very dear to me you were,
> your love to me more wonderful
> than the love of a woman.
>
> How did the heroes fall
> and the battle armour fail?"
>
> 2 Sam 1:23–27

12. David, the Imperfect Image
of the Savior

As soon as Saul was dead, David was made king of Judah, the southern part of the promised land. It took seven years before he was able to dominate the northern section called Israel. After that he ruled the united nation for thirty-three years. His reign was the high point of the Hebrew national history.

One of the first things David did was to march on Jerusalem. The city was so well fortified that it was said the blind and the lame could defend it. But David did conquer it. He went to live in its fortress, which was named the Citadel of David, and made Jerusalem his capital. The capture of Jerusalem completed the centuries-long conquest of the promised land. Even when the kingdom fell apart after David's son Solomon, Jerusalem remained the most important city of the region, and the symbol of Hebrew hopes.

Have you noticed that it was not easy in those days to be a king and remain faithful to God? Can you guess what God did for his chosen son David? God sent him a living conscience. This man was named Nathan: a prophet to express God's will, to call David to task for his misdeeds, and to lead him to repentance.

David had built himself a fine palace of cedarwood. He reflected on the beauty of his palace, thinking, "but God dwells in a simple tent, I must build a temple for Yahweh." When David told him his idea Nathan favored the plan. But that night God gave Nathan some second thoughts, which put David's ambition in perspective and at the same time introduced another dimension of the divine plan for mankind.

God said to David through the mouth of Nathan: "Are you the man to build me a house?"

"Since I brought the Israelites out of Egypt, I have wandered with them living in a tent and I have never asked any of my servants to build me a house. I have made you successful and I have provided a home for my people. I will make you a house." Then God promised that the rule of David's son would last forever.

This prophecy about a son was gradually revealed to mean that the messiah, or savior, was to be a descendant of King David. Mark and Luke refer to this promise in their gospels, and see its fulfillment in Jesus. John describes a discussion about Jesus. One of the unknown speakers says, "Does not scripture say that the Christ must be descended from David and come from the town of Bethlehem?" Jesus puzzled some of his antagonists by asking them: if the messiah were to be David's son, how was it that David also called him "Lord"?

With respect to the other question which arises in this dialogue there was never full agreement about the building of the temple. It was built, but many Hebrews felt it not quite fitting that a God who was everywhere should dwell in a temple. Just before he was stoned to death, Stephen, the first Christian martyr, spoke of King David:

> 'He won God's favour and asked permission to have a temple built for the House (for the God) of Jacob, though it was Solomon who actually built God's house for him. Even so the Most High does not live in a house that human hands have built: for as the prophet says:
> With heaven my throne
> and earth my footstool,
> what house could you build me,
> what place could you make for my rest?
> Was not all this made by my hand?'
> Acts 7:46–50

David's way of acting

In the power struggle after the death of King Saul his many sons and descendants were killed. But David asked, "Is there any descendant of Saul left so I can show him kindness for Jonathan's sake?" Now it happened that Jonathan had a little crippled boy whose nurse smuggled him away and saved him from death when all the rest were killed. There was also a servant of Saul's who had a private work force of fifteen sons and twenty slaves. This servant of Saul's with his team became a very helpful aid to David. He found the crippled son of Jonathan who was brought to share David's royal table and lived at David's court from then on. This was an unusually gracious act on David's part.

David tried to do some other kind acts which were misunderstood. Some of David's political mistakes were the errors of a man too sophisticated and spiritually advanced for his time. You can see this in the events surrounding the death of Absalom, which comes up in a page or so.

David's relationships with women were a source of frustration and trouble to him. His first wife was Saul's daughter, but she was taken away from him. Later he took her back, destroying what appears to have been a happy marriage. This woman was a victim of political considerations, and came to despise David for the wrong reason that he was uninhibited in his worship of God. David married the clever Abigail, widow of a brutal countryman. He married numerous other women and had a large number of concubines besides. Yet, when he was old and ill his servants had to find a young girl to serve him. Gone from David's story is the deep love between man and woman found at the beginning of the Bible.

Possibly David loved Bathsheba, the wife of Uriah, more than any other woman. Who knows? In any case his affair with her occasioned one of the meanest acts of his life. This is what happened.

David's army was away fighting under the command of his general. David himself was in his palace. In the evening he went for a walk on the roof, and from the rooftop he saw a beautiful woman bathing. Her name was Bathsheba. He sent for her, and although he had dozens of wives and she also was married to a man who was away fighting for David, they slept together. She became pregnant. Then David arranged with his general to have her husband put in such a vulnerable position on the front line that he was killed. So he added Bathsheba to his harem.

What David had done displeased God. God sent Nathan, David's living conscience, to tell him a strange parable. Do you know what Nathan said to David?

'In the same town were two men,
one rich, the other poor.
The rich man had flocks and herds
in great abundance;
the poor man had nothing but a ewe lamb,
one only, a small one he had bought.
This he fed, and it grew up with him and his children,
eating his bread, drinking from his cup,
sleeping on his breast; it was like a daughter to him.
When there came a traveller to stay, the rich man
refused to take one of his own flock or herd
to provide for the wayfarer who had come to him.
Instead he took the poor man's lamb
and prepared it for his guest.'

David's anger flared up against the man. 'As Yahweh lives,'
he said to Nathan 'the man who did this deserves to die! He
must make fourfold restitution for the lamb, for doing such a
thing and showing no compassion.'

Then Nathan said to David, 'You are the man. Yahweh the
God of Israel says this, "I anointed you king over Israel; I
delivered you from the hands of Saul; I gave your master's
house to you, his wives into your arms; I gave you the House
of Israel and of Judah; and if this were not enough, I would
add as much again for you. Why have you shown contempt
for Yahweh, doing what displeases him? You have struck down
Uriah the Hittite with the sword, taken his wife for your own,
and killed him with the sword of the Ammonites. So now
the sword will never be far from your House, since you have
shown contempt for me and taken the wife of Uriah the Hittite
to be your wife." . . .

David said to Nathan, 'I have sinned against Yahweh'. Then
Nathan said to David, 'Yahweh, for his part, forgives your sin;
you are not to die. Yet because you have outraged Yahweh by
doing this, the child that is born to you is to die.' Then Nathan
went home.

2 Sam 12:2–15

Nathan said that the child was to die. Although David fasted and
wept, it did die. God was satisfied with David's repentance and
allowed him another son, born to Bathsheba. She named him Solomon. God revealed to His prophet Nathan that He loved Solomon.

[57]

Absalom's revolt

Soon David's numerous sons were fighting among themselves or against their father. Absalom led a revolt so serious that David had to flee for his life. But handsome Absalom was caught in a tree by his own long thick hair. Hanging thus, he was killed by David's chief general Joab. David grieved deeply for Absalom. But his general, Joab, took David to task. Here is the description of the tragic personal dilemma, which shows how even King David was subject to social forces:

> Then the Cushite arrived. 'Good news for my lord the king!' cried the Cushite. 'Yahweh has vindicated your cause today by ridding you of all who rebelled against you.' 'Is all well with young Absalom?' the king asked the Cushite. 'May the enemies of my lord the king' the Cushite answered 'and all who rebelled against you to your hurt, share the lot of that young man.'
>
> 2 Sam 18:31–32

Thus David learned that Absalom was dead.

> The king shuddered. He went up to the room over the gate and burst into tears, and weeping said, 'My son Absalom! My son! My son Absalom! Would I had died in your place! Absalom, my son, my son!' Word was brought to Joab, 'The king is now weeping and mourning for Absalom'. And the day's victory was turned to mourning for all the troops, because they learned that the king was grieving for his son. And the troops returned stealthily that day to the town, as troops creep back ashamed when routed in battle. The king had veiled his face and was crying aloud, 'My son Absalom! Absalom, my son, my son!'
>
> Then Joab went indoors to the king. 'Today' he said 'you are covering the faces of all your servants with shame when they have saved your life today, and the lives of your sons and daughters, of your wives too and your concubines, all because you love those who hate you and hate those who love you. Today you have made it plain that commanders and soldiers mean nothing to you, since now I see that if Absalom were alive today and we all dead, you would be pleased. Now get up, come out and reassure your soldiers, for if you do not come I swear by Yahweh not one man will stay with

you tonight; and this will be a worse misfortune for you than all that has happened you from your youth until now.' So the king rose and took his seat at the gate. All the troops soon heard the news: 'The king' they say 'has taken his seat at the gate'. And the whole army assembled in front of the king.

2 Sam 19:1–9

When David grew old and ill various of his sons competed for the throne. Bathsheba and Nathan encouraged the old man to choose Solomon. He did, and Solomon was anointed. Solomon established his rule with subtle ruthlessness. Of this king the Bible says: "Solomon loved Yahweh: he followed the precepts of David his father, except that he offered sacrifice and incense on the high places." That is to say Solomon committed the sin of idolatry.

13. Idolatry and Injustice
Lead to Disaster

Solomon ruled the Hebrew nation from about 970 B.C. until 922 B.C. He was not a military figure, but a builder of culture. God's special gift to Solomon was wisdom, in the sense of shrewd practicality. He was a wise judge and a creative organizer of businesses and public projects.

It was Solomon who built the temple in Jerusalem, a building designed with care and taste and decorated elegantly. This work left him in debt; he had some difficulties repaying the neighboring king who had supplied the materials and skilled craftsmen. Many of his projects were too costly for the nation to bear. He used slave labor and imposed heavy taxes. These abuses had disastrous consequences and contributed to the division of the kingdom after his death.

But his own days were so much a time of glory that the expression "glory of Solomon" because proverbial. Even Jesus mentioned this slogan, but He mentioned it to say that material glory was not to preoccupy mankind. Jesus said that Solomon in all his glory was not robed as beautifully as the flowers of the field. It is trust in God which is important. Now what about Solomon? Did he set his heart on God?

Unfortunately, Solomon did not. He lacked the righteousness which his father David, despite all his failings, had had. Solomon was not faithful to God. Part of his problem was due to political customs of the time which led him to ally himself with neighboring rulers by taking their daughters as wives. The Bible says that he loved many foreign women. He allowed them to import their customs so that his household of 700 wives and 300 concubines became the scene of alien worship. In his old age Solomon turned to worship one of these imported idols and angered God.

Historical events do not happen suddenly. A real moral decline set in during Solomon's long reign. After his death the nation was torn by civil war for half a century. Until the Babyonian exile, when not suffering from anarchy, Palestine was at best organized into two kingdoms: Israel in the north and Judah in the south. Faith in God declined. The Mosaic Law appears to have been lost for some centuries. Very few of the kings of either Israel or Judah were pleasing in God's sight.

Does this sound like an anti-climax to you? After a thousand years in which God directed His people toward the goal of conquest of the promised land, when they gained it they seemingly lost everything: their unity, their identity, their faith and their land. We will see that in the long run the Israelites did not lose and all mankind gained. But what would you have thought if you had lived then? Keep this question in the back of your mind while we look together at a few of the events of those dark days so long ago.

The worst king of all

The first Book of Kings says that Ahab was the worst king of all. By secular standards, Ahab and his father don't look so bad: they unified the northern area after a long period of anarchy, and built Samaria to be their capital. They were strong enough to be mentioned with respect in the records of the great empires of the time. But from the Biblical viewpoint their reign was an abomination. What did they do wrong? They abandoned God.

Ahab was married to a princess from Tyre on the Phoenician coastland. Her name was Jezebel; her antagonist and God's defender was the prophet Elijah. Jezebel imported hundreds of the priests of the idol Baal. They were supported by the government and a temple to Baal was built in Samaria where King Ahab worshipped. Very few of the people resisted the pressure put on them to worship the idol and abandon God.

God then spoke through the prophet Elijah: a long drought was coming. The famine was so severe that it is mentioned in Phoenician history as well as in the Bible. After warning Ahab, Elijah disappeared. He hid by a stream east of the Jordan where "The ravens brought him bread in the morning and meat in the evening, and he quenched his thirst at the stream."

When this stream dried up God sent Elijah to live with a widow in the town. He met this poor woman gathering firewood at the city gate. All she had to eat was a handful of meal in a jar and a little oil in a jug, but Elijah, the widow and her young son lived on this food until the long drought was over. The jar always had enough meal in it and the oil never ran out. However, at one point the boy almost died. Elijah stretched himself out on the child three times and brought him back to life.

Elijah challenged the prophets of the idol Baal. He and they prepared sacrifices on Mt. Carmel, but did not light them. The idolaters danced and cried all day to their idol to light their wood and burn their sacrifice. But nothing happened. Then Elijah called on God. Fire fell from heaven and consumed his sacrifice. Elijah had the 400 prophets of Baal killed. Then the rains came, ending the drought.

But Jezebel was furious. She was determined to kill Elijah. The prophet fled to the wilderness. There he sat down under a bush and wished he were dead. He said to God, "I've had enough, take my life," and fell asleep. An angel touched Elijah and he woke up. At his head was a jar of water and some bread baked on the hot stones. He ate and drank; strengthened by that food he walked forty days and forty nights until he reached the mountain where God had given the commandments to Moses.

God spoke to Elijah, telling him to anoint three men: two as kings to destroy the Israelites who had turned to idolatry, and Elisha to succeed himself as prophet and leader of the holy war against idolatry.

Elisha followed Elijah, serving the rugged old man with tender love and devotion. Their characters were very different. Elijah was very much of a hermit type, moody and abrupt. Elisha seems to have been gentle and sociable. Neither had a personality suitable to their work of stimulating an extremely cruel and bloody war.

Meanwhile Ahab the bad king had confiscated a vineyard. His wife Jezebel had had the owner stoned to death so that the king could claim it. When Elijah confronted Ahab in the vineyard, Ahab said, "so you have found me out, O my enemy." Elijah told Ahab that all his descendants would be destroyed, which they were. Ahab himself died in battle.

Somewhat later the final event in the story of Elijah took place. It is told graphically in the Bible, so graphically that you almost see and feel it happening:

The brotherhood of prophets who live at Bethel came out to meet Elisha and said, 'Do you know that Yahweh is going to carry your lord and master away today?' 'Yes, I know,' he said 'be quiet.' Elijah said, 'Elisha, please stay here, Yahweh is only sending me to Jericho'. But he replied, 'As Yahweh lives and as you yourself live, I will not leave you!' and they went on to Jericho. The brotherhood of prophets who live at Jericho went up to Elisha and said, 'Do you know that Yahweh is going to carry your lord and master away today?' 'Yes, I know,' he said "be quiet.' Elijah said, 'Elisha, please stay here, Yahweh is only sending me to the Jordan'. But he replied, 'As Yahweh lives and as you yourself live, I will not leave you!' And they went on together.

Fifty of the brotherhood of prophets followed them, halting some distance away as the two of them stood beside the Jordan. Elijah took his cloak, rolled it up and struck the water; and the water divided to left and right, and the two of them crossed over dry-shod. When they had crossed, Elijah said to Elisha, 'Make your request. What can I do for you before I am taken from you?' Elisha answered, 'Let me inherit a double share of your spirit.'. 'Your request is a difficult one' Elijah said. 'If you see me while I am being taken from you, it shall be as you ask; if not, it will not be so.' Now as they walked on, talking as they went, a chariot of fire appeared and horses of fire, coming between the two of them; and Elijah went up to heaven in the whirlwind. Elisha saw it, and shouted, 'My father! My father! Chariot of Israel and its chargers!' Then he lost sight of him, and taking hold of his clothes he tore them in half. He picked up the cloak of Elijah which had fallen, and went back and stood on the bank of the Jordan.

He took the cloak of Elijah and struck the water. 'Where is Yahweh, the God of Elijah?' he cried. He struck the water, and it divided to right and left, and Elisha crossed over. The brotherhood of prophets saw him in the distance, and said,

'The spirit of Elijah has come to rest on Elisha'; they went to meet him and bowed to the ground before him. 'Look,' they said 'your servants have fifty strong men with them; let them go and look for your master; the spirit of Yahweh may have taken him up and thrown him down on a mountain or into a valley.' 'Send no one' he replied. But they so shamed him with their insistence that he consented. So they sent fifty men who searched for three days without finding him. They then came back to Elisha who had stayed in Jericho; he said, 'Did I not tell you not to go?'

2 Kgs 2:3-18

There are three periods in biblical history in which many miracles occured: the time of Moses, the time of Elijah and Elisha, and the time of Jesus. These three times each began a new phase of spiritual development. Moses unified the people, gave them the law as their guide, and set them on their way to the promised land. When they gained this material objective, the Israelites lost their bearings. Where do you go from success, or, as we might say today, where do you go when you are affluent to begin with?

With Elijah, dressed in a hair cloak and a leather loin cloth, eating what the providence of God provided, you have the visual image of the rejection of affluence. With Elisha you have the beginnings of another message: that of personal concern for others. Although not consistently compassionate, there is a striking similarity between some of the miracles performed by Elisha and the miracles of Jesus.

Elisha's miracles

Elisha performed two miracles to provide people with water. In one case he purified the water for a town where the residents were suffering because of bad water. In the other case he provided water for an army so that they could win a victory for God.

Another time he multiplied ten barley loaves and some fresh corn in order to feed one hundred men. Like Jesus when he fed the multitudes by multiplying a few loaves and fishes, Elisha saw to it that the left-overs were collected.

The prophet had friends with whom he stayed when he passed their way, just as Jesus stopped regularly at Bethany. Like Jesus he restored one of his friends to life. However, Elisha's story is not exactly the same as Jesus' restoration of Lazarus. This is what happened in the life of Elisha.

The prophet used to pass regularly by a certain house until the woman who lived there noticed it, and invited him in for a meal whenever he came by. He must have been good company for he never wore out his welcome. After a while the housewife even built him a little room on the roof and furnished it with a bed, a table, a chair and a lamp so he could rest when he came by. He asked her if there was any way he could reward her generosity; she said "No." But Elisha's servant pointed out that she had no children, so the prophet said she would have a son the next year.

After a while, when the child was growing up, a day came when he suffered a sunstroke and died. The mother put her dead child on Elisha's bed, saddled her donkey and rode to Mt. Carmel in search of the prophet. She insisted he return with her.

Elisha sent his servant ahead to revive the child by stretching his staff over him. But this didn't work. So Elisha shut himself in the room. He prayed to God, then lay down on the child putting his mouth to the child's mouth, his eyes to his eyes, his hands on the child's hands. After he had done this seven times the child sneezed! He was breathing again. Elisha also cured a leper. This is how it happened: in a neighboring non-Hebrew country there was an army commander named Naaman who was a leper. His wife had a little Israelite girl as her slave. The little girl told them that the prophet in Samaria, who was Elisha, could cure her master. So the alien army commander went on a formal visit to the Israelite king. He carried a letter from his own king which said, "With this letter, I am sending my servant Naaman to you for you to cure him of his leprosy." When the king of Israel read the letter he was upset. He said, "Am I a god to give life and death?" He thought that his neighbor was trying to pick a quarrel with him by asking him to do the impossible.

When Elisha heard about this he told the king to calm down and send the man to him. So Naaman came to Elisha's door. This is how the Bible tells the story:

> When Elisha heard that the king of Israel had torn his garments, he sent word to the king, 'Why did you tear your garments? Let him come to me, and he will find there is a

prophet in Israel.' So Naaman came with his team and chariot and drew up at the door of Elisha's house. And Elisha sent him a messenger to say, 'Go and bathe seven times in the Jordan, and your flesh will become clean once more'. But Naaman was indignant and went off, saying, 'Here was I thinking he would be sure to come out to me, and stand there, and call on the name of Yahweh his God, and wave his hand over the spot and cure the leprous part. Surely Abana and Pharpar, the rivers of Damascus, are better than any water in Israel? Could I not bathe in them and become clean?' And he turned round and went off in a rage. But his servants approached him and said, 'My father, if the prophet had asked you to do something difficult, would you not have done it? All the more reason, then, when he says to you, "Bathe, and you will become clean".' So he went down and immersed himself seven times in the Jordan, as Elisha had told him to do. And his flesh became clean once more like the flesh of a little child.

2 Kgs 5:8–14

This miracle had a curious aftermath. Elisha refused to take any gift from the man he had cured. Then Namaan declared himself devoted to God, although he had one sin bothering his conscience: when he went with his king to the idol the king worshipped, since the king leaned on his arm, he had to bow with the king to the idol. He asked God to forgive this sin and Elisha answered "Go in peace." And he left.

But Elisha's bungling servant followed Naaman. He wasn't in favor of passing up valuable gifts. So he made up a story about some emergency need, and Naaman gave him silver it took two servants to carry. He hid this money in his house and returned to Elisha.

Elisha asked him where he had been. He said he had not been anywhere. But Elisha knew what had happened. He told his servant that, although he could buy olive groves and livestock and slaves with the money, Naaman's leprosy was transferred to him and his descendants. And the servant became snow white, a leper.

In the miracles worked by Elisha it is noticeable that what we today call miraculous, meaning contrary to nature, and what we call natural, that is, the use of intelligence and keen sense, merge together. The Hebrew people regarded any unusual event as a sign or miracle. They did not divide events as we do. God was behind them all in any case.

Although Elisha performed many signs and did other things in a spirit of compassion he was also behind a brutal war. Nonetheless, on meeting one of the future kings — one of the men Elijah had been told to anoint — Elisha went into what appears to have been a trance and wept at the thought of the horrible destruction to come.

The years of murder and bloody warfare continued long after Elisha's death. Only a few kings were pleasing in God's sight. One of the good kings of Judah, Josiah by name, set about restoring the temple. The workmen found a manuscript which apparently had been lost for centuries: it contained the Mosaic law. Josiah tried to put it into effect but he was too late to restore the moral order. The list of idols he deposed and vices he combatted gives a vivid idea of the degradation into which the Hebrews had fallen. It makes us appreciate how relatively enlightened the Hebrew law was.

Finally in 587 B.C. Jerusalem itself was completely destroyed. The Hebrews who had not already been deported or killed were then deported to Babylon. After a half century of exile a remnant of the Israelites was allowed to return. They found the northern reaches of the promised land occupied by deportees from other corners of the Babylonian empire, and the rest a wilderness.

It took them some centuries to recover a moderate degree of prosperity, and the Hebrews did not redevelop as an independent nation until after World War II, some 2,500 years later, and in our own century. Their development was in another direction: toward the spiritual kingdom. The prophets pondered the meaning of Israel's history and anticipated the most crucial event of all, the coming of Jesus.

14. Prophets Speak

It would seem as if, after God had led His people to the promised land and they had come to possess it securely, then Hebrew history should have ended with the phrase: "and they lived happily ever after." But the chosen people have not lived happily ever after. In fact they have suffered ever since. Was God playing some fantastic joke on them?

During the centuries of disorder after Solomon, the Hebrews meditated deeply on their new situation. Many prophets, true and false, arose to explain this failure of success. The true prophets were God's instruments. God sent them to guide His chosen people. The true prophets flattered no one, often made the rulers angry, and were, some of them, killed. You have already seen how Elijah, the first of the prophets (not counting Moses and Aaron) spoke fearlessly in the name of God.

The early prophet Amos shattered many illusions of the people. He told the Israelites to stop fooling themselves: the glorious future had a dark side and would be a time of judgment. God was not going to give the Israelites everything or anything unless they lived upright lives. God demands justice. He demands that each man serve his neighbor and care for the poor. Foolish Israelites may think that they can hide their sins behind rituals, but God is not to be deceived. God will destroy His faithless people, saving only a few. Here are some passages from the book of Amos which sum up these ideas:

> Trouble for those who are waiting so longingly for the day of Yahweh!
> What will this day of Yahweh mean for you?
> It will mean darkness, not light,

[68]

as when a man escapes a lion's mouth,
only to meet a bear;

Seek good and not evil
so that you may live,
and that Yahweh, God of Sabaoth, may really be with you
as you claim he is.
Hate evil, love good,
maintain justice at the city gate,
and it may be that Yahweh, God of Sabaoth, will take pity
on the remnant of Joseph.

Am 5:18–19, 5:14–15

The prophet Amos also pointed out that God was the ruler of all nations, not only the Hebrews:

Are not you and the Cushites [Ethiopians] all the same to me,
sons of Israel? — it is Yahweh who speaks.
Did not I, who brought Israel out of the land of Egypt,
bring the Philistines from Caphtor, and the Arameans from Kir?
Now, my eyes are turned on the sinful kingdom,
to wipe it off the face of the earth.
Yet I am not going to destroy
the House of Jacob completely — it is Yahweh who speaks.

Am 9:7–8

Amos' poem goes on to say that God is going to be especially hard on those smug sinners who say "no misfortunes will ever touch us." In the end God will rebuild "the tottering hut of David." Because the prophets constantly make a connection between the future savior and the family of David, the fact that Jesus was descended from David is an important link between the Old and New Testaments.

Prophetic expression

Amos was one of the twelve minor prophets — those whose writings are short. The quotes above are clear and fairly simple for us to understand. Not all the prophetic writings are so easy for us to read. Many of the prophetic books contain poems which are full of symbolism and references which are meaningless to us. Some of the meaninglessness results simply because we do not live where they lived: remarks about Chicago or Washington would have meant nothing to them, and remarks about Moab and Cush mean nothing to us. Some other difficulties are due to the transmission and translation of manuscripts over thousands of years. Some of the difficulties stem from the ancient literary genre, so full of what we would call exaggerations, black and white contrasts, symbolism and cryptic names for certain places and persons. And some of the difficulty was because the authors were trying to express the almost inexpressable.

The prophets used a rich variety of images and their expressive techniques were often extremely vivid. One prophet, Hosea, made his whole life situation an image of the situation of Israel. Hosea was married to a woman who was not faithful to him, so he described God as being married to the faithless bride Israel. Hosea hoped for a better future: he said that God loved his people so much that someday he would restore them.

While Hosea expressed God's message in terms of the common experience of marriage, another prophet, Ezekiel, did just the opposite. He saw human experience as a sort of surface behind which angels and heavenly armies were active. His visions seem very fantastic to us and his expressions extravagant, but he also believed that God would someday restore His people and give them a new spirit.

Can you guess how this man with a terriffic visual imagination put the same thought about the restoration of God's people which Hosea had seen as the return of a faithless wife? Ezekiel said that one day he and God walked together around a valley full of dry bones. Then God ordered Ezekiel to breath on the bones and the bones stood up on their feet and became living persons, an immense army. There is a gay American spiritual about Ezekiel's vision of the dry bones. Do you know it? It is usually called "O' Dem Dry Bones."

Another great prophet, Jeremiah, who lived right at the time Jerusalem was destroyed and the Hebrews were exiled to Babylon, agreed with Hosea, Ezekiel and the other prophets, in denying that God had completely abandoned His people, but he expressed his hope for the future differently:

> See, the days are coming — it is Yahweh who speaks — when I will make a new covenant with the House of Israel (and the House of Judah). . . .

Deep within them I will plant my Law, writing it on their hearts. Then I will be their God and they shall be my people. There will be no further need for neighbour to try to teach neighbour, or brother to say to brother, 'Learn to know Yahweh!' No, they will all know me, the least no less than the greatest — it is Yahweh who speaks — since I will forgive their iniquity and never call their sin to mind.

Jer 31:31–34

The prophet who drew a portrait of the savior

One of the longer prophetic books in the Bible is that of Isaiah. It does not all appear to be by the same author, but was written by two or more authors who lived two centuries apart. At least this is what the scripture scholars think at present. Within the last few years a complete text of the book of Isaiah, much more ancient than any other now in existence, was found near the Dead Sea in Palestine. When this old manuscript has been studied thoroughly, scholars may understand the book better. Even if the book of Isaiah had several authors who lived in different centuries there is enough unity of thought and an exceptional beauty of expression in the whole book to hold it together.

Isaiah had a vision of God as a king seated on a high throne surrounded by six-winged angelic creatures who cried out "Holy, holy, holy." Isaiah's first reaction to this vision was to think with horror of his own sinfulness and unworthiness to see God. Then one of the angelic creatures took a burning coal and touched it to Isaiah's lips to purify him. From then on his only thought was to be of service to God.

When Isaiah heard God asking, "Who will be our messenger?" he replied, "send me." Jesus quoted this part of the book of Isaiah some eight centuries later, saying that Isaiah's words were being fulfilled by his, Jesus', life and the reactions of people to His mission. Here is the whole dialogue from the sixth chapter of Isaiah:

Then I heard the voice of the Lord saying:
 'Whom shall I send? Who will be our messenger?'
I answered, 'Here I am, send me'. He said:
 'Go, and say to this people,
  "Hear and hear again, but do not understand;
  see and see again, but do not perceive".

[71]

> Make the heart of this people gross,
> its ears dull;
> shut its eyes,
> so that it will not see with its eyes,
> hear with its ears,
> understand with its heart,
> and be converted and healed.'
>
> Is 6:8–10

The prophecies of Isaiah applied to his own period in history. But the Gospels also apply them to Jesus. It is the seventh chapter of Isaiah which contains the prophecy about the birth of Immanuel, or "God with us," recalled in the description of Jesus' birth.

Jesus, himself, quoted what is called "Second Isaiah." This part of the book of Isaiah describes the coming savior as the suffering servant of God. Jesus identified Himself as this suffering servant. Here are a few of the many lines of poetry in which Isaiah tells of God's chosen one, the savior:

> I, Yahweh, have called you to serve the cause of right;
> I have taken you by the hand and formed you;
> I have appointed you as covenant of the people and light of
> the nations,
> to open the eyes of the blind,
> to free captives from prison
> and those who live in darkness from the dungeon.
>
> Is 42:6–7

Admittedly the Bible does select out of the more general context of history, the events which show how God and man relate. Still the way God's plan unfolds and the way events fit together over such long stretches of time is fascinating. The members of the early Christian community understood the exceptional relevance of the prophecies of Isaiah to the life of Jesus. Apparently Jesus had taught His disciples to see this connection, and they were able to explain it to others. So we find the deacon Philip, within a few years after the death of Jesus, using the words written some six centuries before Jesus, about the suffering servant who was to come, to make one of the first Christian converts of central Africa! Here is the story from the eighth chapter of the Acts of the Apostles:

The angel of the Lord spoke to Philip saying, 'Be ready to set out at noon along the road that goes from Jerusalem down to Gaza, the desert road'. So he set off on his journey. Now it happened that an Ethiopian had been on pilgrimage to Jerusalem; he was a eunuch and an officer at the court of the kandake, or queen, of Ethiopia, and was in fact her chief treasurer. He was now on his way home; and as he sat in his chariot he was reading the prophet Isaiah. The Spirit said to Philip, 'Go up and meet that chariot'. When Philip ran up, he heard him reading Isaiah the prophet and asked, 'Do you understand what you are reading?' 'How can I' he replied 'unless I have someone to guide me?' So he invited Philip to get in and sit by his side. Now the passage of scripture he was reading was this:

> Like a sheep that is led to the slaughter-house,
> like a lamb that is dumb in front of its shearers,
> like these he never opens his mouth.
> He has been humiliated and has no one to defend him.
> Who will ever talk about his descendants,
> since his life on earth has been cut short!

The eunuch turned to Philip and said, 'Tell me, is the prophet referring to himself or someone else?' Starting, therefore, with this text of scripture Philip proceeded to explain the Good News of Jesus to him.

Farther along the road they came to some water, and the eunuch said, 'Look, there is some water here; is there anything to stop me being baptised?' He ordered the chariot to stop, then Philip and the eunuch both went down into the water and Philip baptised him. But after they had come up out of the water again Philip was taken away by the Spirit of the Lord, and the eunuch never saw him again but went on his way rejoicing.

Acts 8:26–39

PART TWO:
THE NEW TESTAMENT

15. Jesus Christ

In the first part of the Bible, the Old Testament, knowledge of God was brought to mankind by many, many different persons and events. Each added a part to the development of an increasingly complete picture. In the New Testament the entire revelation comes from Jesus Christ or is interpreted as coming through Jesus. Jesus Himself reveals God, so much so that to know Him is to know the Father. The different writers and the activities undertaken by Jesus' followers develop and deepen human understanding of Jesus. Before Jesus, men grew in their readiness for His coming. After Jesus men also grow, but "in Him" in order to become more like Him, the first born of the new creation.

Do you know how many years have passed since the birth of Jesus Christ? It is easy to tell since our years are numbered from Jesus' birth. Have you ever asked what this could mean? Does it not mean that we live in the time of the new creation?

History is divided into two great periods with Christ as history's axis and division. When our calendar was invented the intention was to arrange all history around its center, the life of Christ, beginning with His birth. But (and maybe you didn't know this) an error was made in the calculations. Jesus was born sometime before the date which the calendar assigns, at least four years, and perhaps as many as eight years, "before Christ." No one knows on what day of the year Jesus was born. December 25 has been celebrated as His birthday for many centuries.

During most of His life Jesus lived as an ordinary unknown Hebrew villager in the northern part of the promised land. Palestine was then ruled by the Romans. Jesus lived according to the customs of the people and the Law of Moses. He kept the old feast days of the Israelites and prayed in the words of the psalms. His attitude toward the Roman overlords was contractual: when Roman things, such as their money, were used, then the Romans were entitled to their return. His views were revolutionary, but at a deeper level than political revolutions which do not go beyond the rearranging of who is first and who is last and how they relate. He said that the first *would* be last and that the suffering and cast-off members of society were blessed.

For most of His life Jesus was so anonymous a person among the anonymous common folk that people were astonished when He became a traveling rabbi, or teacher. People asked, how did He learn to read and write? How did He come by such powers? Isn't He just one of us, a village lad, the son of Mary and Joseph?

Jesus' mother was named Mary. Her position in the plan of salvation is unique. The longest expression of her thoughts given in scripture is the poetic "magnificat" in which she praises God for His merciful love for humble people. The ideas it contains are similar to Jesus' teachings about the blessedness of the faithful poor as contrasted with the proud and wealthy. Mary seems to have become more and more involved with Jesus' work as time went on. She was with Him when He died and with the apostles when the Spirit came upon them and the Church was born.

It is assumed that Mary's husband, Joseph, died before Jesus began His active public life, since Joseph is last mentioned in scripture when Jesus was twelve years old. When Jesus was near death on the cross He asked John, His beloved disciple, to care for Mary, so it is quite clear that Joseph was dead or he would have been caring for her. The Gospels say of Joseph that he was a just man. To be a just man sums up perfection: Joseph was faithful to God and charitable to men. The little said about him gives a remarkable amount of information about his character. We know enough about Joseph from the stories about Jesus's birth and childhood to give us a picture of a man of profound faith, integrity, genuineness, independence of judgment, boldness, sensitivity and love.

Joseph, Mary, and Jesus probably lived with a big group of relatives and not alone as we almost always see them in paintings. It was normal in Hebrew society for groups of brothers and sisters, grandparents, cousins and even what we would call distant relatives to live together. All those of the same generation called each other brother and sister.

We don't know what Jesus' occupation was but there weren't very many possibilities. He probably cared for sheep as a boy and may have been a carpenter as a young man. Jesus did not marry. Most men, then as now, did marry, but the Bible never suggests that His remaining unmarried was abnormal in His society. Jesus affirmed the right of men to remain unmarried for the sake of the kingdom of heaven, and Paul later applied this to women, freeing them from what many people then felt to be an obligation.

When Jesus was about thirty years old He went to be baptized by the prophet John, one of His more distant kinsmen. This began His public life as a preacher of the word of God. Most of the New Testament is about the period of probably three years between His baptism and His death. Jesus then revealed that the kingdom of God had at last come in His own person. The event which established the kingdom and was crucial in every respect was His death and resurrection.

How did it happen that Jesus died? His death puzzled believers since it seemed to contradict the revelation that the savior was to reign forever. Looking at His death from the outside, it was not so extraordinary. His teachings antagonized the established powers, and, as has happened to so many reformers in history and is still happening today, the authorities found some excuse, held a false trial, and had Him killed. Jesus did not resist death but accepted it as His God-given vocation. He did die. His body was hastily enbalmed and put in a tomb.

Paul said that the death and resurrection (or coming to life again) of Jesus was the central, crucial event on which all else hinged. The other apostles and disciples agreed. In saying this, Jesus' followers were echoing the thought he himself expressed from time to time, more and more urgently, during His public life.

For Jesus foresaw His death: like a magnetic pole attracting a compass, it was the focus guiding His life. He puzzled His followers with remarks about His time not having come yet, and the day of His presence ending. On the last night of His ordinary human life He prayed that God might find a less difficult alternative, but not without saying that the will of his Father, God, was all that mattered. Usually Jesus looked forward to His death with deep joy because it was the Father's will, and was His vocation or the key to His personal reality, and because it was going to reconcile mankind with God.

The rest of the Good News depends on the death and resurrection of Jesus. Some parts of the Gospel message have to do with who Jesus was. Other parts tell us how to follow Jesus and be united with Him in His new life. Sometimes we learn from scripture what to avoid as anti-Christ, or how to deal with ourselves. All this is good and useful only if Jesus really died, rose again, and thus reconciled mankind with God. Christians know that he did rise from the dead and that He is living right now.

Three days after Jesus died (counting in the inclusive way of ancient peoples) He became alive again. He met with His followers in a number of different places. He ate with them and talked with them. Then Jesus left them, rising from the earth before their eyes.

Jesus' frightened, bewildered followers stayed more or less together until God's Spirit, whom Jesus had promised to send, came upon them and converted them into new men, without fear, the first citizens of the new creation. In one of its earthly, imperfect and incomplete expressions, this new creation, or the kingdom of God, is the Christian Church. This Christian Church produced the second part of the Bible, called the New Testament (or New Witness or New Covenant). More important, it leads men and women to grow in likeness to Jesus.

The New Testament

The New Testament consists of four accounts of Jesus' ministry, a book about some of the experiences of the Christian Church, letters by followers of Jesus, and a book of a visionary nature about the problems facing the first Christians.

The four accounts of Jesus' ministry are called Gospels. The word Gospel means good news. These books are not biographies, but tell about what Jesus did and said from the point of view of revelation, that is, in order to make God known to men. Three of these are very similar and are called the Synoptic Gospels. They are the Gospels of Matthew, Mark and Luke.

The other Gospel contains many details not recorded by the three Synoptic Gospels. This last is called the Fourth Gospel and seems to have been written at least a generation or two after the other three. Tradition says that John was its author. Many people take this to mean that he was the source of its information while others doubt the tradition altogether. The quesion of the authorship and sources of all four gospels is a complicated one which scholars are gradually resolving. But whatever the scholars decide does not effect the value of what the gospels in fact contain. They contain authentic information about God and His love for mankind. The scholars do help us to understand the meaning of what was written, but they do not make the gospels true or false.

Luke is also the author of Acts, a history of the early Church. This history is not complete. It does not tell us what all of Jesus' followers did but only about some things which happened immediately after Jesus' death before His followers scattered, and then about the journies of a few of the apostles. A large part of Acts is about the travels of Paul.

The longer letters which form an important part of the New Testament were written by Paul. They are letters to churches he founded or planned to visit. Some short letters by other apostles are also included in the Bible.

The final visionary book is traditionally said to have been written by John, although it is less likely his than the Gospel assigned to him. It is called Revelation, or the Apocalypse. Regardless of who wrote it, its ideas are in harmony with the other books and it adds another dimension to our understanding of God.

These writings were by people who were in contact with Jesus or else companions to those who knew Him. When the generation of those who knew Jesus was dead no more writings were added to the Bible. Jesus had completed the reconciliation of man with God so the record of God's dialogue with men ended formally when the recollections of those who had immediate contact with Jesus ended. Now men meet God living in the members of His Church, though many who go by Christ's name do not reflect His teachings.

What God has inspired men to write since revelation was completed is dependent on the Old and New Testaments. However, men are still growing in their understanding of God. Paul already distinguished in his letters his own opinion as distinct from what the Lord Jesus had revealed, so God's saving activity continues. You and I are called to realize it in our lives.

16. The Kingdom of God and the Law

Jesus spoke with authority. In His actions, in His teaching, in His ways of relating to people He ignored trival social rules, which the "establishment" of scribes, pharisees and elders were bent on enforcing. Thus His behavior was a real challenge threatening to them.

Mark tells us that some members of this establishment complained directly to Jesus one day, but He put them off. He asked them what they thought about John's baptism. They were afraid to say that John's baptism came from God, for then the people would ask them why they had not accepted it. On the other hand these leaders were afraid to depreciate John in front of people who believed that he was a real prophet. So they said they didn't know and Jesus said He wouldn't answer their questions since they would not answer His.

Jesus then told a parable, that is, a story in which both the different elements and the entire pattern of the story can be matched with some other series of events. In this parable a man planted a vineyard and leased it to some tenants. The parable can be read as a summary of the history of Israel in which the Israelite leaders are the tenants or agents of God (the owner) in caring for His vineyard (the chosen people). The prophets are the servants God sent, whom they abused. The established leaders saw the criticism of the evil tenants as directed at themselves. Here is Jesus' parable. See if it is as clear to you as it was to the Hebrew establishment:

> He then proceeded to warn them in parable style: "Once upon a time a man planted a vineyard, set up a fence round it, dug a vat, and erected a tower. He then leased it out to

vinedressers and went abroad. In due time he sent an agent to the vinedressers to receive from them a share of the vintage. They seized and beat him, and sent him back with empty hands. So he sent to them another agent; but they struck him on the head and insulted him. Yet another he sent, and this one they killed; and so they treated many others, beating some and killing others. He still had a beloved son, whom he sent to them last of all, saying: 'They will respect my son.' But those vinedressers said to one another: 'This is the heir; come, let us kill him, and the inheritance will be ours.' They laid hold of him, killed him, and threw him out of the vineyard. What, then, will the owner of the vineyard do to them? He will return, and put the vinedressers to death. Yes, and he will give the vineyard to others!"

Mk 12:1–10

While we are looking at this parable I want to show you something. Maybe you are tuned in to what I have in mind, and maybe not. The thing is that this story is terribly real. The behavior of the leaders is the behavior that drives us crazy every day. People just seem to be blind to the options they are given. If the Hebrew leaders had believed the parable — and they did believe the threat it contained — they *could* have taken the option of accepting God's son and reversing the consequences. Today we have situations like race riots which white people don't want. Prejudiced white people know perfectly well that if they really and completely abandoned their racial prejudices and stopped noticing what color people were when they applied for jobs and moved next door, then race riots wouldn't happen, but they won't take the option. Neither will people take the options they know to be real about arms, about the development of poor countries, about trade and many other things. This is the same kind of phoniness which eroded the ancient establishment which put Jesus to death.

The Bible is not interested in pulling morals of this sort out of its events, but tells its stories straight, as descriptions of reality and of the acts of God. A moral is an interpretation of an event from the point of view of some problem or question in the mind of the person viewing the event. Because the Bible is so real it lends itself to the exposing of problems, problems of yesterday, today and tomorrow. You can call this moralizing — not a bad thing if we know what we are doing — and something we do all the time although we frequently fool ourselves into thinking we are doing something else.

This way of reading things is also suggested by Jesus' teaching method, the parable. Some of the Jesus' parables are re-enacted every day, such as the one about the good Samaritan, and others can be compared with current events to help us see these events more sharply. It's OK to do this so long as we don't think the biblical writer was solving our problems for us: we have to solve our own problems but the Bible can help us see them clearly.

Let's see how the vineyard parable applied to the ancient Hebrews. God built a good and productive vineyard and gave it to a chosen people to cultivate it for Him. Instead the chosen people rejected His dominion. It's the same old story: Adam and Eve rejected God's dominion and thus lost the paradise God had given them to cultivate. So the infidelity of the chosen people was to lead to the loss of their special relationship with God. In particular, the son's death was to lead to the end of the old order of things for those whom God had set apart, protected and cultivated to serve Him.

However, God does not usually end good things by discarding them, but by transforming them into something better. The son is to die, yes, but with his death a new creation is to begin. Or you could say that the original "good" creation is restored. In any case, the vineyard is not abandoned but transferred to new cultivators who will be faithful. The son and heir establishes a deeper relationship with God than the relationship formerly established through human agents. As Jesus said, speaking of John the Baptist, the least person in the Kingdom of Heaven (born of the Spirit) is greater than the greatest prophet, John, of the old, exclusively human (born of woman) creation.

Did Jesus give any clues about the future friends of God? Who are to be the heirs of God's loyal servants, the prophets of old, and of His Son? They are those persons who are faithful to God, and like the prophets and His Son, endure persecution for the sake of God the Father and His Son. Jesus said, "Happy are you when people abuse you and persecute you and speak all kinds of calumny against you on my account. Rejoice and be glad, for your reward will be great in heaven; this is how they persecuted the prophets before you."

Jesus used the mountain slopes as His classrooms. Teaching the people who sought Him out, He said to them, "Do not imagine that I have come to abolish the Law or the Prophets. I have come not to abolish but to complete them." Nothing is to be lost of the Law, which guided the chosen people in the ways of God, *until its purpose is achieved.* Those persons who obey the commandments have a high place in the kingdom of heaven (which is also called the kingdom of God and the new creation).

On the other hand, Jesus said to the people that if their virtue did not greatly surpass that of the scribes and pharisees (Hebrew leaders of Jesus' time) then they would never get into the kingdom of heaven. Jesus also said, ". . . unless you change and become like little children you will never enter the kingdom of heaven." And He said it would be hard for a rich man to enter the kingdom of heaven. Jesus talked constantly about the kingdom of heaven and compared it to a wedding feast, daily work, a mustard seed and many other things in order to make known different aspects of this central idea.

But what else did He say on the mountain about the kingdom of heaven and the Law? Following Matthew's Gospel, this is what He said: It is not enough not to kill: a man must not even become angry with his neighbor. It is not enough not to commit adultery: a man must not even desire to do so in his heart. It is not enough to fulfill oaths: leave off swearing and be honest all the time by making your "yes" mean "yes" and your "no" mean "no." It is not a question of an eye for an eye and a tooth for a tooth (which is what the Law of Moses said), but do not resist the wicked man. Let the wicked abuse you; give to anyone who asks anything of you. It is not sufficient to love your neighbor and hate your enemy: you must love your enemies. "You must therefore be perfect as your heavenly Father is perfect." You are made in God's image: become what you are.

Where are the new people of God to be found? On whom does God's blessing descend? Who are the happy children of the kingdom of heaven? Jesus found them everywhere, on the highways and on the byways, in the crowded towns and alone by village wells, among the wealthy occasionally but more often among the poor, among Romans, pagans, converts and Jews. As Paul later said, in the heavenly kingdom all the world's divisions count for nothing. Here is the explanation Paul gave to the Galatians (the people in one of the churches he founded) of the relationship between the chosen people and the citizens of the new creation established by Jesus:

> Before the faith came, we were in the custody of the Law, held captive while waiting for the faith that was to be revealed. In this way the Law has been our attendant on the way to Christ, that we might be sanctified by faith. But now that the faith has come, we are no longer under the care of the attendant. You are, in fact, all children of God through faith in Jesus Christ, since all of you who have come to Christ by baptism have clothed yourselves with Christ. No longer is there Jew or Greek; no longer is there slave or freeman; no longer is there male or female. You are all one in Christ Jesus. And if you are Christ's, then you are the offspring of Abraham, heirs according to the promise.
>
> Gal 3:23–29

This is how Jesus spoke to those people who were open to His message and journeyed, thoughtless even of eating, to listen to Jesus' words:

> One day when his eyes fell on the crowd, he went up a mountainside, where he sat down, with his disciples close to him. Opening his lips he gave to his hearers a lengthy instruction, saying:

> "Blessed are the humble souls,
> for theirs is the kingdom of heaven.
> Blessed are the meek and gentle,
> for they will inherit the land.
> Blessed are the sorrowing,
> for they will be consoled.
> Blessed are those who hunger and thirst after holiness,
> for they will be fully satisfied.
> Blessed are the merciful,
> for they will have mercy shown to them.

Blessed are the singlehearted,
for they will see God.
Blessed are the promoters of peace,
for they will rank as children of God.
Blessed are the victims of persecution for conscience' sake
for theirs is the kingdom of heaven.

Blessed are you when you are reviled, or persecuted, or made
a target for nothing but malicious lies — for my sake. Be joyful
— leap for joy; a rich reward awaits you in heaven. So, too,
were persecuted the prophets who preceded you."

Mt 5:1–12

17. Jesus' Hour

Early in His public life, at Cana, Jesus made an odd sounding remark. He was talking to His mother, Mary, and said, "Woman, why turn to me? My hour has not come yet." Then Jesus did change water into wine, His first miracle so far as we know, but He did not explain what He meant by "hour has not come yet."

Later on, just before His death, Jesus said, "Now the hour has come . . ." He meant the hour for the accomplishment of His mission, and in particular His death. Jesus spoke of His passion, death and resurrection as the hour in which God would glorify Him. He also said this was to be the hour of darkness and of the power of the devil, and an hour He, Jesus, would just as soon skip if God gave Him an alternative.

The words Jesus said are often quoted: "Father, if you are willing, take this cup away from me. Nevertheless, let your will be done, not mine." Here the word "cup" sums up the suffering and death Jesus was about to undergo. Jesus also spoke of the "cup" of the new covenant God was making with mankind through His death. This new covenant was prepared for by the old covenant God had made with Moses, or rather, with mankind through Moses. These are the words which the gospel reports Jesus to have said: "This cup is the new covenant in my blood which will be poured out for you."

There is a lot of symbolic expression here. Symbolism is a sort of short-hand. It points to lots of different dimensions of reality all at once, and says more than simple declarative sentences can say. Do you know what I think: I think you really can take symbolism because you're open to reality.

Jesus talked about His "hour" as if it alone was going to make His life real. In this hour all mankind is caught up together with Jesus Christ at the core of the mystery of life itself. This is the hour of mankind's birth into the new creation, the death which makes rebirth possible. This is what Jesus said:

> "Come at last is the hour for the Son of Man to be glorified! I tell you the plain truth: unless the grain of wheat fall into the earth and die, it remains just one grain; but once it has died, it bears abundant fruit."
>
> Jn 12:23-24

Jesus' death is the single death, like the death of the seed, when it is planted in the earth, which will produce much fruit, much growth. Jesus went on to explain this idea and to show how men and women can become united with him in his fruitful death:

> "He who holds his life dear destroys it; he who sets no store by his life in this world will preserve it for eternal life. Whoever would be in my personal service must follow me; and then, wherever I am, there, too, my servant will be. Whoever is in my personal service will be honored by the Father."
>
> Jn 12:25-26

This same idea is repeated and developed in all four gospels. Probably Jesus repeated these paradoxical sayings over and over. Here is a passage on the same theme from Matthew's gospel:

> Then Jesus said to his disciples: "If anyone wants to become my follower, he must renounce himself and shoulder his cross; then he may be a follower of mine. Indeed, he who is bent on saving his life, must part with it anyway; but he who freely parts with his life for my sake will secure it in the end. Clearly, what will it profit a man to gain the whole world when his life is forfeited in any case? Or, what price can a man pay down to purchase life forever? Furthermore; the Son of Man is to come hereafter wrapt in his Father's glory and escorted by his angels; and then he will repay everyone according to his conduct."
>
> Mt 16:24-27

After these thoughts, which show how mankind is related to Jesus' life and death, the Gospel according to John goes on to explain many aspects of Jesus' death, at length and very beautifully. Jesus' "hour" is for the glory of God. This "hour" is also a time of judgment. This hour will end the hold that the devil has on mankind:

> "Now is the sentence of condemnation being passed upon this world; now is the prince of this world being evicted; and I, once I have been lifted up from the earth, will draw all men to myself."
>
> Jn 12:31–32

To those who join themselves with Jesus by believing in Him, God the Father will give a new life in the new creation. A few things are revealed about this new eternal life: for one thing it won't negate life as death does, but will be more real than the life with which we humans are familiar, because death will have been overcome. The life of heaven will be a life full of variety, as Jesus put it, "having many mansions" or place for everybody according to the character of each. Heaven will also be a place of personal relationships, especially personal relationship with Jesus. It will not have "marriage" which is an institutional relationship but it will be the place where the love of which marriage is an image will be fulfilled. Of course, "place" is a poor word to use about heaven as was illustrated by Jesus after the resurrection. He moved around rather freely with respect to place appearing here and there, walking through walls, rising above the earth. But the passage to this joyful, active and creative eternal life is through death. The death of Jesus was the turning point for all mankind. How did Jesus die?

"Kill him"

The establishment of the chief priests and scribes had made up their minds to kill Jesus from just about the first moment of His active life. These men were institutional leaders, or organization men, of the common type which tends to put control over others and the continuation of the organization in place of the purpose for which it and their own positions exist. Anyone who by-passes their control is a threat to them. And Jesus by-passed their control.

This is one of the more significant aspects of Jesus' behavior which His imitators down through the centuries have often overlooked. Obedience is directed to God. Jesus and the apostles taught this. It should seem rather obvious, even apart from Jesus' example of persistent dissent, that since men are fallen, sinful and alienated from God, obedience to men can involve disobedience to God. Jesus also made it clear that responsibility is universally distributed, so that no one can displace his personal responsibility to obey God.

Each man and woman must subordinate, or reject, if necessary, all other so-called obediences. On one occasion Jesus told some people to obey the establishment, but not to imitate the persons in the roles of leadership. He frequently defied them Himself, and made a point of breaking their "blue laws" or the legalistic formalisms which oppressed people and falsified religion.

Jesus' own obedience to the authorities was not a simple obedience. With respect to His death, He did not have to meet, or confront the authorities at all. He did not have to go up to Jerusalem from His camp at the Jordan. But Jesus *chose* to confront them so that they could carry out their instrumental role in God's plan. God used these officials even to the point of putting words into their mouths as he had once put words into the mouth of Balaam and his donkey. Thus the high priest remarked prophetically that one man should die for the people. Pilate exposed the fundamental conflict with his question, "what is truth?"

Jesus made it clear that He was complying with God and not with any of these human instruments. God was using these men to contribute to the fulfillment of His plan; Jesus didn't even feel He should speak to them except insofar as it served to clarify God's work.

During His life Jesus explained many times that people are their own judges. People are not saved or condemned before God by an exterior act of God but by their own interior life and the behavior which comes out from this inner man or woman. This idea is very much in evidence in the events connected with Jesus' death: for everyone involved His passion and death was a "crucial experiment" in self-judgment. Most of Jesus' words were comments on how people were judging themselves and placing themselves relative to the new creation, from Judas who destroyed himself (better that he had never been born) to the thief whose sincerity won him a place in paradise (today you will be with me in paradise).

Jesus' enemies found their opportunity to act against Him at the time of the Passover feast. The Passover was a memorial of the Exodus and the covenant with Moses. Paralleling passage from the worldly land of Egypt to the promised land, Jesus passed from this world to the kingdom of God. Paralleling the limited covenant which anticipated His coming and prepared some people to receive Him, came the covenant which is with all mankind and fulfills the human hope for total life.

It was while Jesus was eating the Passover meal with His twelve apostles that He told them one of them was going to betray Him. Jesus said, "Yes the Son of Man is going to his fate as the Scriptures say he will, but alas for that man by whom the Son of Man is betrayed! Better for that man if he had never been born!"

The betrayer, Judas, left the dining room, apparently after this warning. He led a group of the establishment's thugs to a place where Jesus could be captured without causing a public uproar. This scheme worked because Jesus allowed it to work. The biblical texts show that Jesus was in command of every detail of the passion events. This is not in itself odd. Any intelligent man, knowing the people and social circumstances, could have anticipated the behavior of the people involved. Jesus went regularly to Gesthemane, the quiet garden just outside the town of Jerusalem. He was captured there. It was the obvious place. If Jesus had been dodging capture He could have gone someplace else that evening.

Every moment of the weekend of Jesus' death had an unparalleled intensity. Each of the four Gospels captures this intensity in a different way. The nearly 2000 years of Christian history have been an unfolding and a probing of the meaning of that weekend.

The Last Supper

It was at the same Passover supper we were talking about above that Jesus gave Himself to all men under the forms of bread and wine. Jesus asked that His union with mankind be recalled forever and gave to everyone a realistic sign of this union. This is how the first communion is recorded in Mark's Gospel:

Before supper was over, he took bread into his hands and, after saying grace, broke it into portions, which he gave them with the words: "Take it! This is my Body." He also took a cup and, after saying grace, passed it on to them and everyone drank of it. He said to them: "This is my covenant-blood, which is about to be shed for the sake of many. I tell you truly, I shall never again drink of the product of the vine till that day when I drink new wine in the kingdom of God."

Mk 14:22–25

These communion words are given in each of the three Synoptic Gospels, with very slight variation. Matthew mentions "for the forgiveness of sins," and Luke adds, "do this as a memorial of me." Paul describes the same event in his first letter to the Corinthians. Through his remarks we learn about the life of the early followers of Christ and about how they made this communion central to faith, calling it the "Lord's Supper."

John's Gospel does not give the same details. Instead, John attributes other sublime words to Jesus, which may be interpreted as a commentary on the communion. The events connected with Jesus' death have special mystery; it is John who probes further dimensions of this mystery. Of course, we are always surrounded by mystery: take our own growth from chromosomes, or the rising of the sun, or the turning on of the radio, or the way words tie to things. But the key salvation events — the Last Supper, Jesus death by crucifixion, His return to life, and His free departure from earth — these events have more levels of mystery than men have yet dreamed of.

Jesus said, "this is my body" and "this is my blood." Did Jesus mean the "thisness" to apply to the objects involved or the group activity of doing this, or both together? How far did Jesus want the thisness He spoke of to extend? Jesus was then in the room in His human, before-death body when He spoke of "my body." He indicated the particular bread in His hands and wine in His cup: Christians have generalized this to use bread and wine of many types and sources in conjunction with the words Jesus spoke, as the matter, so to speak, of their memorial suppers. The active thisness, "do this" has been variously interpreted and even sepa-

MATTHEW

If the ancient traditions are correct, then the Gospel which goes by the name of Matthew was written by one of the twelve apostles. The story of Jesus' call to this apostle is given in the Synoptic Gospels. Matthew was also called Levi. He was a customs official which meant he had to be able to read and write in Greek as well as in Aramaic. Aramaic was the language of Jesus and his companions. The Gospel of Matthew which we have was written in Greek but there is an old tradition that it was first written in Aramaic. The Greek Gospel seems to date from about 80 A.D. It is thought that it was written for Christians of pagan origin, non-Jews, because it shows a special interest in the salvation of the pagans.

rated from the "thisness" of Jesus in the objects, the bread and wine. Is the recalling of Jesus' death automatic or do people need to know about it and think of it to make the supper mean anything? What do you think about these questions? Or, if you think they don't matter, why don't they matter?

When Jesus ate with His twelve founders of the Christian community, and gave them His body to eat by sharing bread with them, He was also in the midst of His body in another sense which Paul later explained. Paul spoke of Jesus' faithful friends as His mystical body. Jesus Himself had said that where two or three were gathered in His name He was among them. But at the Lord's Supper this mystical body was with Him in the persons of the twelve, who relate to the Christian people as the twelve patriarchs related to the Israelites. This was His body: the living community united with Him. This is the body John talks about in his gospel. John integrated the ideas symbolized by the wine (the product or fruit of the vine), and by the community. This is what John tells us Jesus said at the Last Supper:

> "I am the real vine, and my Father is the vinedresser. He prunes away any branch of mine that bears no fruit, and cleans any branch that does bear fruit, that it may bear yet more abundant fruit. By now you are clean, thanks to the lessons I have given you. Remain united with me, and I will remain united with you. A branch can bear no fruit of itself, that is, when it is not united with the vine; no more can you, if you do not remain united with me. I am the vine, you are the branches. One bears abundant fruit only when he and I are mutually united; severed from me, you can do nothing. If one does not remain united with me, he is simply thrown away like a branch, and dries up. Such branches are gathered and thrown into the fire to be burned."
>
> Jn 15:1–6

The trial

The place where Jesus was captured by His enemies was a garden outside the Jerusalem city walls. He got there early for His "appointment" with His enemies. During the interval Jesus prayed with deep feeling. His abandonment by His closest followers was foreshadowed in their inability to stay awake to pray with Him. Jesus told them how they were going to behave. He told Peter in particular that Peter would even deny knowing Him.

Jesus was indistinguishable from other men, so that Judas had to point Him out. Judas chose to point Jesus out by kissing Him, apparently a normal enough greeting. Jesus was no touch-me-not at all as some Christians seem to have thought, but shared sleeping quarters and common dishes and used ordinary expressions of affection with His friends. He had to reassure the people sent to capture Him that He was, in fact, the man they wanted.

Then His followers deserted Jesus. Peter, however, followed the group which took Jesus to the high priest's palace. This is the first trial as Mark records it, perhaps from Peter's description, and the story of Peter's cowardice.

They led Jesus before the chief priest, and all the chief priests, the elders, and the Scribes assembled. Peter, meanwhile, had been following him at a distance all the way into the palace of the chief priest, where he loitered among the guards, warming himself in the glow of the fire.

Now the chief priests — in fact, the Supreme Council as a body — were looking for testimony unfavorable to Jesus in order to have him put to death; but they did not find any. Many, it is true, had testified falsely against him, but their testimony did not agree. Finally, some stood up and, falsely testifying against him, said: "We ourselves have heard him say: 'I can tear down this sanctuary made by the hands of men,' and, 'Within three days, I can build up another not made by the hands of men.'" And thus, again, their testimony did not agree!

Then the chief priest rose in full view and asked Jesus: "Have you nothing to say in your own defense? What about the evidence these men are furnishing against you?" But he remained silent, and said nothing in his own defense. Again the chief priests asked him: "Are you the Messias, the Son of the Ever Blessed?" "I am," replied Jesus; "moreover, you are going to see the Son of Man enthroned at the right hand of the Almighty and coming wrapt in the clouds of the sky."

The chief priest tore his garments and said: "What further need have we of witnesses? You heard the blasphemy! What is your verdict?" They all voted him liable to the penalty of

[97]

death. And now some made free to spit on him and blindfold him and slap him in the face and say to him: "Play the prophet!" Even the guards struck him with the open hand.

While Peter was in the courtyard below, one of the chief priest's servant girls came and, catching sight of Peter, who was warming himself, looked straight at him and said: "You were with Jesus the Nazarene." But he denied it. "I do not in the least understand what you mean," he said. He then went out into the gateway, and a cock crowed. There the servant girl noticed him and, in turn, made herself busy saying to the bystanders: "This man is one of them!" But he again denied it. After a little while the bystanders for their part said to Peter: "You are certainly one of them; why, you are a Galilean!" Then he burst out cursing and swearing: "I have nothing to do with this man you are talking about." And immediately, now for the second time, a cock crowed. Then Peter recalled the prediction — how Jesus had said to him: "Before a cock crows twice, you will disown me three times." And he broke out into sobs and tears.

Mk 14:53–72

This first trial of Jesus took place in the middle of the night. Of course, it was not a trial in any legitimate sense of the word. Neither did this group of Hebrew officials, the Sanhedrin, have any civil power. They could not carry out a death sentence. Their first move in the morning was to take Jesus to the Roman official who could execute people under the civil code.

This Roman governor, Pilate, was the epitome of all the bad ideas associated with the word "politician": a sponge as far as principles and justice were concerned, ready to soak up the views opportunism might suggest. He wanted to keep everybody satisfied with the least disturbance of the status-quo. When Jesus was brought before him, he played with everyone involved, bringing out their positions so as to make it appear that he could not have done anything other than what he did do, and thus to dodge making a proper decision.

Mark's Gospel does not record his effort to pass the buck to Herod. To get the full picture all the Gospels have to be put together. But these adversaries of Jesus, dime-a-dozen types we can unfortunately read about every day in our current newspapers, are not our primary concern. We are seeking Jesus, the positive expression of life. This is the rest of the record of Jesus' execution from Mark's gospel:

Finally, Pilate, desiring to satisfy the mob, released Barabbas as their choice, and had Jesus turned over for a scourging preliminary to crucifixion.

The soldiers then led him away into the interior of the palace, that is, the praetorium, and called together the entire cohort. They clothed him in a purple cloak, and put on him a plaited crown of thorns. Then they proceeded to salute him: "Long live the King of the Jews!" They also struck his head with a reed, and spat on him, and paid him homage on bended knees. When they had done making sport of him, they stripped him of the purple cloak and dressed him in his own clothes. Then they led him out to be crucified.

They compelled a certain Simon of Cyrene, the father of Alexander and Rufus, who was passing by on his return from the country to carry his cross. They led him to a place called Golgotha, which means "Skull's Mound." Here they offered him drugged wine; but he did not take it. Then they crucified him. His clothes they divided among them by drawing lots for them, to see what each one was to get.

It was nine in the morning when they crucified him. There was also the usual inscription stating his guilt: "The King of the Jews." Together with him they crucified two bandits, one at his right, the other at his left. Thus the Scripture was fulfilled which says: "He was classed with lawless men."

Meanwhile the passers-by kept insulting him. They shook their heads and said: "Bah! You are the one that can pull down the sanctuary and build it up in three days!" "Save yourself and come down from the cross!" The chief priests joined the Scribes and said in the same taunting manner to one another: "He saved others! He cannot save himself!" "Let the Messias, the king of the Jews, come down from the cross this instant: we want to see and believe!" And they who were crucified with him, reviled him.

About noon darkness fell upon the whole land and lasted till three o'clock. At three o'clock Jesus cried out with a strong voice: "Eloi, Eloi, lama sabachthani," which means: "My God, my God, why do you abandon me?"

Some of the bystanders who heard it, said: "Listen, he is

calling for Elias." Then someone ran and soaked a sponge in sour wine and, putting it round a reed, offered him a drink, saying: "Let me see whether Elias is coming to take him down." Jesus uttered a loud cry and expired.

Then the curtain of the sanctuary was torn in two from top to bottom. When the centurion, who stood by facing him, saw that he had expired under such circumstances, he said: "This man was really the Son of God."

Also women were present, looking on from a distance. Among them were Mary Magdalen, Mary the mother of James the Younger and of Joseph, and Salome. They had accompanied him and ministered to his wants while he was still in Galilee. Besides these, there were many others who had come up with him to Jerusalem.

It was now late in the afternoon. And because it was the Day of Preparation, that is, the eve of the Sabbath, Joseph of Arimathea, a councilor in good standing, who was himself waiting for the kingdom of God, came and made bold to interview Pilate in order to petition for the body of Jesus. Pilate was surprised that he was already dead. So he sent for the centurion and asked him whether he was already dead. On learning the facts from the centurion, he made Joseph a gift of the body. Joseph took him down and wrapped him in the linen shroud which he had bought, laid him in a tomb which had been cut out of the rock, and rolled a stone against the entrance of the tomb. Mary Magdalen and Mary, the mother of Joseph, carefully noted where he was laid to rest.

Mk 15:15–47

18. I Am the Resurrection

Nowadays there are many theories about what Jesus thought of Himself. In general, the scholars say we do not and can not know since it was His followers who put down what they remembered and found useful to support their faith. In this book we are not going to think about these theories since they are too complicated and uncertain. Someday you may want to look into them. But, in reading this book, please, remember that we are taking the Bible at face value though not entirely literally, and that this is *not* the only way to read the Bible. It is however, a useful way and a way to begin even if it is "out grown" later.

According to the Gospel of John, Jesus raised His good friend Lazarus to life again after Lazarus had died and had been buried four days. At that time Jesus said to Lazarus' sister Martha:

> "I am the resurrection and the life, . . . he who believes in me will live even if he dies; and no one that lives and believes in me shall be dead forever."
>
> Jn 11:25–26

Could it be that Jesus, who had said these words and had brought His friend Lazarus back to life, was Himself dead and gone forever? No. What then? The Bible tells us that Jesus died. It also tells us that He returned to life, both to a normal life in which He was indistinguishable from other travelers along Palestine's roads, and ate and talked, and to a rather extra-normal life in which He passed through closed doors, asked not to be touched at least for the moment, and finally rose from the earth to disappear among the clouds.

[101]

The parts of the New Testament which deal with the resurrection, or coming-to-life-again, of Jesus, are among the most complex in scripture, even at face value. Jesus' meetings with His friends cannot be put into one simple sequence. Many different types of people, social customs, legal procedures and physical circumstances contributed to these events.

Did Jesus die?

Some people have claimed that Jesus did not die. According to the Bible His enemies certified that He did die. A squad of Roman executioners nailed Jesus to a cross so He would die either by bleeding or suffocating. Two thieves were crucified at the same time; just a routine day's work for the executioners. The place of execution was public and there were many witnesses. Pilate made an enquiry about Jesus' death and was assured by his officer, a centurion, that Jesus was dead. The leaders of the Jews had already told Pilate that Jesus was dead, but he mistrusted them and asked his own official to be sure. He also sent a squad to remove the bodies. These soldiers finished killing the two thieves by breaking their legs but found Jesus already dead. One of them drove a lance into His side which drew blood and water. All these indifferent or enemy types agreed that Jesus was dead.

His friends took Him for dead too. They hastily buried Him in a nearby tomb. They observed the Hebrew Sabbath restrictions and the women among them prepared to embalm His body on the following day, our Sunday.

Now there is a significant difference between the testimonies about Jesus' death, and those about his appearances alive again after His death. After Jesus returned to life He was seen only by His followers. Paul mentions an occasion when Jesus was seen by more than 500 people, but even this big group seems to have been made up of disciples. Most of Jesus' appearances were to one or two people, or to the apostles as a group.

Jesus' new life

The first appearances of Jesus after His death were to some of His women followers. They went to the tomb in which Jesus' body had been hastily placed. They found it empty but were told by angels to return to the apostles and tell them that Jesus had risen. According to Matthew the whole group of women met Jesus. John's Gospel is a little different, though not necessarily in disagreement with Matthew's:

They had not as yet understood the Scripture text which says that he must rise from the dead. The disciples then left for home.

Mary, meanwhile, had been lingering outside the tomb, weeping. As she was giving vent to her tears, she stooped to look into the tomb, and saw two angels dressed in white, seated where the body of Jesus had lain, one at the head, the other at the feet. "Good woman," they said to her, "why are you weeping?" "Because," she replied, "they have taken away my Master, and I do not know where they laid him!" With this, she turned round to look behind and saw Jesus standing by, but did not know that it was Jesus. "My good woman," Jesus said to her, "why are you weeping? Who is it you are looking for?" Taking him for the gardener, she replied: "Sir, if you carried him away, tell me where you laid him. I want to remove him." Then Jesus said to her: "Mary!" Turning round, she said to him in Hebrew: *"Rabbouni!"* which means "My Master." "Do not hold me any longer," Jesus said to her; "I have not yet ascended to the Father; go therefore to my brethren and say to them: 'By and by I will ascend to my Father and your Father, to my God and your God.'" Mary Magdalen went to carry the message to the disciples. "I have seen the Master!" she said, and that he had told her so-and-so.

Jn 20:9–18

Jesus appeared several times to the apostolic group. John tells the intriguing story of Thomas' doubt and also brings out a problem Jesus seems to have had with His apostles. From the beginning to the end of the Gospels Jesus constantly has to tell his followers not to be afraid. "Fear not," "peace," "do not be afraid," "why are you fearful?" — over and over Jesus had to calm down and strengthen His followers. In Luke's version of this incident more emphasis is put on their fright than in John's Gospel, but let us read it in John's version:

Late in the evening that same day — the first day of the week — although the doors of the place where the disciples had

[103]

gathered were bolted for fear of the Jews, Jesus came and stood before them, and said: "Peace be to you!" With that, he let them see his hands and his side. The disciples were delighted to see the Lord. Then Jesus said to them again: "Peace be to you! As the Father has made me his ambassador, so I am making you my ambassadors." With this, he breathed on them and said: "Receive the Holy Spirit. Whenever you remit anyone's sins, they are remitted; when you retain anyone's sins, they are retained."

Thomas, one of the Twelve, called the Twin, was not with the group when Jesus came. So the other disciples said to him: "We have seen the Master!" But he replied: "Unless I see in his hands the print of the nails, and put my finger into the place where the nails were, and lay my hand into his side, I am not going to believe!"

Eight days later, his disciples were again in the room, and Thomas was with them. Jesus came, though the doors were bolted, and, standing before them, said: "Peace be to you!" He then addressed Thomas: "Let me have your finger; put it here, and look at my hands. Now let me have your hand, and lay it into my side. And do not be incredulous, but believe!" Then Thomas burst out into the words: "My Master and my God!" "Because you have seen me," Jesus said to him, "is that why you believe? Blessed are those who have not seen and yet believe!"

Jn 20:19–29

All the descriptions of Jesus' post-resurrection encounters with His friends are fascinating: how Jesus walked toward Emmaus with two of His friends, how He found the apostles out fishing, and finally the descriptions of the ascension. We cannot include them all in this book. You can find them at the end of each Gospel. But here is the final paragraph from the Gospel according to Matthew:

As for the eleven disciples, they betook themselves to the mountain in Galilee to which Jesus had ordered them. When they saw him, they adored him, although at first they had doubts. Jesus then came closer to them and spoke to them the following words:

"Absolute authority in heaven and on earth has been conferred upon me.

Go, therefore,
and make all nations your disciples:
baptize them in the name
  of the Father
  and of the Son
  and of the Holy Spirit,
and teach them to observe
all the commandments I have given you.
And mark:
I am with you at all times
as long as the world will last."

Mt 28:16–20

Now that we have learned about Jesus' death and resurrection we can look back and reflect on His life. Who was this Jesus of Nazareth? What did this great prophet tell us?

The descriptions of Jesus' birth have to do with the question, who was this man? They also give us a picture of the variety of relationships different men and women have with Jesus. They teach us a number of lessons about growth in holiness.

Jesus was born of God. All men and women are born of God and all children are His gift, but Jesus was born of God in a very special sense. Through Him God's glory is made known and made present among men. Hidden things, as Jesus said, are revealed to little ones. Through Jesus God opens His arms to welcome His poor servants who put all their trust in Him.

In John's Gospel Jesus' birth is seen in a cosmic way which relates all creation to Jesus' life on earth. John speaks of Jesus as God's Word, or wisdom, who shared in the original work of creation and later came into the world to make God known and loved. Here is John's description of Jesus, the Word of God:

> Meanwhile the true light,
>> which illumines every man,
>> was making its entrance into the world.
> He was in the world,
>> and the world came to be through him,
>> and the world did not acknowledge him.
> He came into his home,
>> and his own people did not welcome him.
> But to as many as welcomed him
>> he gave the power to become children of God —

those who believe in his name;
who were born not of blood,
    or of carnal desire,
    or of man's will;
    no, they were born of God.
And the Word became man
    and lived among us;
    and we have looked upon his glory —
    such a glory as befits
    the Father's only begotton Son —
    full of grace and truth!

Jn 1:9–14

The birth of Jesus

Each evangelist has his own way of expressing Jesus' unique relationship with God. Throughout history people have found the way used by Matthew and Luke to be especially meaningful. These two writers told about Jesus' human birth. Their stories contain the same information, but there are differences too. Matthew, for example, tells of Jesus' conception from the point of view of Joseph. Here is Matthew's text:

Regarding the conception of Jesus Christ, this is how it happened: his mother Mary had been espoused to Joseph; but before they lived together, it was found that she was pregnant by the Holy Spirit. Joseph, her husband, being right-minded and unwilling to expose her, resolved to put her away without public formalities. He had just made up his mind to this course when an angel of the Lord appeared to him in a dream and said: "Joseph, son of David, do not scruple to take Mary, your wife, into your home. Her conception was wrought by the Holy Spirit. She will bear a Son and you are to name him Jesus; for he will save his people from their sins." This event with all its circumstances was to fulfill the Lord's prediction made through the prophet, who says:
    "Behold! The virgin will be pregnant
        and give birth to a Son,
        who will be called 'Emmanuel' " —
which means "God with us."
    After awaking from his sleep, Joseph did as the angel of the Lord had directed him, and took his wife into his home.

He had no conjugal relations with her before she gave birth to a Son, whom he named Jesus.

Mt 1:18–25

There is an old tradition that Mary, Jesus' mother, told Luke what she remembered about Jesus' birth. This is quite possible. The tradition is based on Luke's comment that, like a good news reporter, he searched out well-informed people to check the information in his gospel. Since Mary was one of the members of the early Christian community, he may have been able to talk his writings over with her. He seems to have some details which only she could have known and sometimes even says what her feelings were.

No one has the means at present to prove or disprove this old way of piecing hints together. Many people also view the entire text from a less realistic point of view, not as in any sense an historical happening, but as a symbolic image of the spiritual realities in which the Christian community was interested.

It is Luke who tells most of the details about Jesus' birth. According to Luke the angel Gabriel told Mary that she was to be the mother of the savior, who would be born to her even though she had no sexual relations with any man. Thus this birth was an act of God's will, independent of man's will. Nonetheless, the child was to be the descendant of David and thus fulfill the prophecies about him. Mary accepted these acts of God as one of God's faithful poor.

The angel had also told Mary that her aged kinswoman Elizabeth was pregnant and awaiting the birth of a child. This part of the angel's announcement was a sign, confirming the idea that nothing was impossible for God to do. Mary set out immediately to stay with Elizabeth until Elizabeth's son, John the Baptist, was born.

Mary

We meet Mary from time to time throughout the Gospels. Whenever we meet her she is active and traveling far from her home for some purpose. The picture of her which piety and art have constructed in recent centuries is not found in the Gospels. While it cannot be proven that she did not stay at home alone praying and spinning, the Gospels tell us she was where the action was. She traveled a lot: to Egypt, up to Jerusalem for feasts, to neighboring towns for weddings or to help relatives like Elizabeth, and seems

[108]

toward the end of Jesus' public life to have joined the group of women who traveled around with Jesus, caring for Him and His followers. She was at Jesus' side when He was crucified, and not because someone sent her a telegram to tell her to fly down. She was very much a part of the apostolic band.

It may be that Jesus' remark to Mary just before His death on the cross should be interpreted, not as a request to John to care of her, but the other way round: perhaps Jesus meant her to be John's helper, since John seems not to have had a wife to travel with him and care for him as Peter and most of the other apostles did.

Even the story of Jesus' birth as recorded by Luke gives us a picture of a going and spiritually growing person. Here is what Luke tells us about Jesus' birth and the shepherds who were invited by God's angels to welcome His Son:

Long before that day a decree had been issued by order of Caesar Augustus that a census of the whole world should be taken. This census was the first to take place while Cyrinus was in charge of Syria.

Accordingly, the people went, each to the city of his ancestor, to be registered; and so Joseph, too, being a member of the house and family of David, went up from the town of Nazareth in Galilee to David's town in Judea, called Bethlehem, in order to be registered. He was accompanied by his espoused wife Mary, who was with child. In the course of their stay there, the time came for her delivery; and she gave birth to her first-born son. She wrapped him in swaddling clothes, and laid him in a manger, because there was no accommodation for them in the lodging.

In the same region shepherds were camping in the open and keeping watch over their flocks by night. Suddenly, an angel of the Lord stood facing them, and the glory of the Lord shone round about them, so that they were struck with terror. "Do not fear," the angel said to them. "Listen: I am bringing you good news of great joy which is in store for the whole nation. A Savior, who is the Lord Messias, was born to you today in David's town! And this will serve you as a token: you will find an infant wrapped in swaddling clothes and cradled in a manger." All of a sudden, the angel was joined by a crowd of the heavenly host, praising God with the strain:

"Glory to God in the heavens above,
and on earth peace to men of good will."

When at last the angels had withdrawn from them and returned to heaven, the shepherds said to one another: "Let us go over to Bethlehem and find out the truth about this thing the Lord has made known to us." So they set off in haste, and sought out Mary and Joseph and the infant cradled in a manger. And when they saw them, they made known what had been told them about this little child. All those who heard the account given them by the shepherds expressed surprise, while Mary treasured all these incidents and meditated on them in her heart. At last the shepherds returned, glorifying and praising God for everything they had heard and which afterwards was seen to be just as they had been told.

Lk 2:1–20

The shepherds

It seems to me that the story of the shepherds captures the whole movement of revelation and response which we meet in scripture. Ordinary men, who trust in God, are granted a vision. Angels spoke to the early patriarchs, now angels speak to their descendants. What do the angels tell them? That the savior has finally come, but that they have to go and seek him out. They are given signs by which to recognize Him. They respond by going. They find what they have been told to expect. They share the information the angels had given them, impressed by the exact fulfillment of prophecy. They recognize and accept Jesus. Thus they pass from the Old Testament witness of anticipation to the New Testament witness to Jesus' presence among men. They return to their daily life and work as men converted, witnesses to the breaking through of the new (or renewed) creation. After the resurrection Jesus commanded His followers to proclaim the gospel to every creature. The shepherds anticipated this mission.

The actions of Herod contrast with those of the shepherds. He also was told of Jesus' coming, but instead of going to adore the savior and to learn more, Herod sent his agents to destroy the child, and wound up deceived and fooled, with a futile and despicable series of murders to his name.

The Magi, like the shepherds, were among God's chosen friends.
They seem not to have been Hebrews, neither were they poor, but
they watched the signs of the times and hoped for God's revelation.
Thy related to the men of their own time as scientists relate to our
society today, in fact, our sciences and scientists are the heirs of
countless alchemists' and astrologers' efforts over the centuries. Like
good empiricists these men consulted the evidence of nature. When
they lost sight of the natural sign, the star, they consulted political
and religious leaders. They found Jesus and rejoiced. Then they
were warned in a dream; their understanding of men and things
told them of Herod's animosity to Jesus, so they went home to their
own country by a different route. Wise and free they moved about
as conscience directed them. This is the story of their visit as told
by Matthew:

> After Jesus was born at Bethlehem in Judea, in the days of
> King Herod, a commotion arose in Jerusalem when Magi from
> the East arrived and inquired: "Where is the newborn King
> of the Jews? It was his star we saw in the East, and we came
> to offer homage to him."
>
> The news threw King Herod into consternation, shared by
> all Jerusalem. Assembling the whole body of the chief priests
> and Scribes — the nation's Council — he inquired of them where
> the Messias was to be born. "At Bethlehem in Judea," they
> said to him; "for this is what has been written by the prophet:
>> 'And you, Bethlehem, in the land of Juda,
>> are not the least of Juda's principalities;
>> for out of you shall come forth a Ruler,
>> who will shepherd my people Israel.'"
>
> Then Herod secretly summoned the Magi and, after care-
> fully ascertaining from them the time during which the star
> had been visible, he sent them to Bethlehem with this injunc-
> tion: "Go and make careful inquiries about the child, and,
> when you have found him, report to me. I, too, wish to go
> and do homage to him." So they obeyed the king and went
> their way; and, unexpectedly, the star they had seen in the
> East preceded them till it came and stopped over the place
> where the child was! At sight of the star they were supremely
> happy. And so, entering the house and seeing the child with

his mother Mary, they threw themselves down to do homage to him. Opening also their treasure chests, they presented him with gifts: gold, frankincense, and myrrh. But advised in a dream not to return to Herod, they departed for their country by a different way.

Mt 2:1–12

There are three more steps in the path of prophecy: Herod tries to kill Jesus and instead kills a number of innocent children; Joseph takes Mary and Jesus to Egypt, and the family ultimately returns and settles in Nazareth in northern Palestine. All these actions fulfill scripture and contribute to Jesus' mission. It is Luke, however, who completes the information which we have about Jesus' early life. He describes the dramatic events which happened when Joseph, Mary and Jesus went to the Temple to fulfill the legal rituals connected with the birth of a child. Then he tells us that the child grew to maturity in Nazareth, giving us a glimpse of Jesus at the age of twelve. You can read these very beautiful descriptions of Jesus' early life in Luke, chapter 2, verses 22 to 52. Perhaps you will be surprised by the last sentence in which Luke sums up Jesus' childhood: "And Jesus increased in wisdom, in stature, and in favor with God and men."

20. The Greatest Man of the Old Creation

One day, when John the Baptist was in prison, Jesus spoke to John's followers. He spoke about the man they loved and admired. John, said Jesus, was greater than all the other prophets. All the prophecies of the prophets and the law led to John. John was the messenger sent to prepare for the immediate arrival of the savior.

The close relationship between John and Jesus makes the life story of John, which is fascinating in itself, even more interesting to us. Probably you know already that John was beheaded during a party and that his head was presented on a dish to a dancing girl. The gory details about how he died as a victim of human corruption would not be so intriguing to people were he not, himself, so noticeably the opposite of his murderers. John was a person of unique integrity, absolutely faithful to an extraordinary, God-given vocation. Let's see if we can put together the information about the Baptist which is scattered throughout the four Gospels and come to know this man whom Jesus loved.

Many Old Testament themes are repeated in the life story of John. He was a child of promise given by God to an aged, childless couple. John's father, Zechariah, was a Hebrew priest. The angel Gabriel spoke to Zechariah when he was carrying out his priestly role in union with the prayer of the devout Hebrew people. Through the angel, God promised Zechariah so special a son that He said beforehand what his name was to be and how he was to live.

Like Abraham, Zechariah found the promise of a child hard to believe. For his doubt he was temporarily struck dumb. Zechariah's

[113]

wife Elizabeth also shared in the revelation from God, perhaps partly through her kinswoman Mary, the mother of Jesus. After the same angel, Gabriel, had spoken to Mary, she had gone to stay with Elizabeth. Their encounter was an occasion for divine inspiration. Mary seems to have stayed with Elizabeth until John was born.

Before John's birth, Elizabeth as well as the still-dumb Zechariah knew that the child was to be called John. In fact, she had an argument with their relatives about it when the time to name him arrived. They were all set to ignore her when Zechariah backed her up by writing "John" on a tablet. At that same moment Zechariah's speech was restored. He spoke in poetry, blessing God and saying of his new born infant:

> And you, my little one, will be hailed
> 'Prophet of the Most High';
> for the Lord's precursor you will be
> to prepare his ways;
> you are to impart to his people
> knowledge of salvation
> through forgiveness of their sins.
> Thanks be to the merciful heart of our God!
> A dawning Light from on high will visit us
> to shine upon those who sit in darkness
> and in the shadowland of death,
> and guide our feet into the path of peace."
> Lk 1:76-79

John the Baptist's way of life

It was predetermined that John was to live as a prophet. John's fearless initiative, which ultimately led to his death, shows that he developed his vocation. He lived what is called an ascetical life: a life of poverty, prayer and self-discipline. He drank no wine and ate the locusts and wild honey which he found in the desert wilderness. He dressed in a rough cloth of camel's hair held together by a leather belt.

John baptized people with a baptism of repentance. He preached the immediate coming of the savior. A group of followers gathered around this great man. John's followers imitated his severe life. Later on people criticized the followers of Jesus for not fasting like the followers of John. Jesus said that His followers were not fasting because they had the joy of His presence with them, but that they would fast when He had gone away. Jesus also remarked that critics are never satisfied: they blamed John for fasting and Jesus for not fasting.

At the Jordan River John baptized those who came to him. They entered into the water of the river as an external sign of their sorrow for their sins. John knew that the baptism he offered was of limited power, but that it was a step in the direction of the more powerful reconciliation with God that the savior was about to offer.

John and Jesus

Jesus' followers adopted the rite of baptism. Jesus, the source of the baptism of the Spirit, never baptized anyone with water Himself. I wonder why?

Jesus took the ministry of John the Baptist as the point of departure for His own active, public ministry. The two men, Jesus and John, had a thorough understanding of the dynamics of their missions and their mutual relationship. Both understood that Jesus was to increase and John was to decrease, that is, contribute to Jesus work and then diminish in significance and lose his following to Jesus.

It is interesting that John did not seem to have a foreknowledge of Jesus' identity. There is an inconsistency with the infancy stories here. John said, "Someone is following me, someone who is more powerful than I am, and I am not fit to kneel down and undo the strap of his sandals. I have baptized you with water, but he will baptize you with the Holy Spirit." John waited for God to identify the savior with a sign. When Jesus came to be baptized the sign was given. John identified Jesus as the savior for whom he was making people ready. From then on he said of Jesus, "This is the one of whom I said: He who comes after me ranks before me because he existed before me."

The sign by which John recognized Jesus was an expression of the Triune God. When Jesus, God's Son, entered the water to be baptized, John saw the Spirit in a visionary way which is described as "like a dove." This is what the other John, the author of the fourth Gospel, records:

[115]

The following day he say Jesus coming toward him. "Look,"
he said, "there is the lamb of God, who takes away the sin
of the world. This is he of whom I said: 'There is a man to
follow me who takes precedence over me because he existed
before me.' I, too, had not known him; but he had to be
made known to Israel, and it is for this purpose that I came
to baptize with water."

Now, John testified as follows: "I have seen the Spirit coming down in the shape of a dove from heaven; and he rested
upon him. I, too, had not known him, but he who sent me
to baptize with water also said to me: 'If you see the Spirit
come down upon someone and rest upon him, that is the one
who baptizes with the Holy Spirit.' Therefore, as an eyewitness
I declare: This is the Son of God."   Jn 1:29–34

The Synoptic Gospels add a further detail, in the words of Matthew: "And a voice spoke from heaven, 'This is my Son, the Beloved; my favour rests on him'" (Mt 3:17).

According to the fourth Gospel it was from among the Baptist's
disciples that Jesus found His first followers. When Jesus passed by
one day, John told these men to look at Jesus, for Jesus was the
lamb of God. So they followed Jesus and spent the whole day talking with Him. One of these men was Andrew; he brought his
brother Peter to Jesus. Peter became the leader of Jesus' followers.
The Baptist was content to contribute the men he had prepared to
Jesus' following. He recognized and accepted this as his mission.

Do you know what John taught men in order to prepare them
for Jesus' coming? Fortunately, apart from the general idea of being
sorry for sins, we do have a bit of "how" and "what" from John's
teaching as it is given in Luke's gospel:

"What, then, are we to do?" he answered them as follows:
"He who has two tunics should give one to him that has
none; and he who has food should do likewise." Also tax col-
lectors came to be baptized by him. "Rabbi," they said to him,
"what are we to do?" "Exact nothing," was his answer to
them, "in excess of the rate prescribed to you." Also men of
the police force consulted with him. "And for our part," they
said, "what are we to do?" He replied: "Browbeat no one;
blackmail no one; and be content with your pay."

Lk 3:10–14

MARK

At the end of his first letter, Peter adds greetings from his son Mark. In the book of Acts we find the apostles meeting in the house of Mary and her son Mark. Both these references are thought to be to the author of the Gospel according to Mark. Mark is also identified with the cousin of Barnabas who traveled with Paul. If these traditions are true then Mark was certainly in a central position in the early Christian community. Scholars who lived in the second and third centuries say that Mark was Peter's traveling companion and that he wrote his Gospel in Rome just after Peter died. Peter was killed in one of Nero's persecutions, but it is not certain whether in 64 or in 67 A.D.

Jesus' teachings included these ideas taught by John. However, the content of Jesus' teaching was generally more radical. There is one aspect of Jesus' teaching which may seem strange to us. This is the way in which it was related to prophecy. When Jesus returned to His home town he went to the synagogue (the local Hebrew house of prayer) and opened the writings of the prophet Isaiah to a passage about Himself. In this prophecy Isaiah said that the savior would bring good news to the poor, proclaim liberty to captives, bring new sight to the blind, and set free the downtrodden. Remember this.

Now when John was imprisoned, just before his death, although he had already identified Jesus as the savior, he sent two of his followers to Jesus for confirmation of his identity. Can you guess how Jesus answered their question? Jesus had just cured many people of illnesses and deformities. He said to John's followers:

> "Go and bring word to John about all you see and hear: the blind recover sight, the lame walk, lepers are made clean, the deaf hear, dead men rise again, the humble have the Good News preached to them"; and, "Happy the man to whom I am not a stumbling block!"

Lk 7:22

John was perhaps closer in spirit to Jesus than anyone else, even closer than Peter, John, Mary Magdalen and the family at Bethany. Mary, His mother, was probably closer although there are passages in the Gospels in which Jesus appears to be distancing Himself from her, but on the other hand she is more taken for granted than rejected even in these passages. If the poem Mary said to Elizabeth is any indication, Mary was of one mind with Jesus and John the Baptist. At the end she is shown to be very close to Jesus.

Jesus was deeply moved by the death of John the Baptist. The Gospels show us that Jesus tied His prayer to events which happened, although there is reason to think He observed the Hebrew prayer routines also. Jesus was in the habit of praying either alone or with one or two companions before entering into important activities, and when He was face to face with difficult situations. When Jesus heard of John's death, He took His followers with Him to a lonely place. However, people followed them and Jesus healed them, multiplying loaves and fishes for them to eat. When He could, when He had completed his services to the multitude, He went on to do what He had first intended when He went into the lonely wilderness: He slipped away into the hills to pray.

Jesus said of John: "John came to you, a pattern of true righteousness, but you did not believe him . . ." (Mt 24:23) and another time, "I tell you, of all the children born of women, there is no one greater than John; yet the least in the kingdom of God is greater than he is" (Lk 7:28).

21. Prayer

So large a part of the Gospels is about prayer that it is hard to select the little bit we have room for in this book. Jesus was a reformer of prayer. Praying was something He found being done badly at the time He lived. Since men relate themselves to God through prayer, Jesus was especially interested in purifying prayer. About the only violent thing Jesus is recorded to have done was to throw the money changers out of the house dedicated to prayer and the worship of God.

In ancient times people used to pray out loud, that is, they said all their personal prayers out loud, as well as the common prayers groups of people say together. When the holy woman Hannah prayed to herself (on an occasion recorded at the beginning of the books of Samuel) the priest accused her of being drunk. Instead, our Lord Jesus encouraged people to pray by themselves, privately and in secret, but Jesus also prayed out loud many times. When Jesus told people to pray privately He was teaching them what sort of confidence they should have in God and what sort of honesty they should have about prayer.

One time Jesus told a story about two men who were praying side by side. One of these men saw himself as utterly poor and inadequate before the perfection and goodness of God. He asked God to show mercy to him and to overlook his sinfulness. The other fellow saw himself as well-off and more or less congratulated God for having made someone so admirable as himself. He even thanked God for having blessed him more than He had blessed the poor man praying beside him. His idea of God was so insensitive that we shudder at it. Still it is hard to be free of his defects. Jesus said that this proud man's prayer was unacceptable to God, while the prayer of the humble man pleased God.

The trouble with the noisy prayer was that it wasn't what it pretended to be, adoration of God and a loving dialogue with Him. It was not directed toward honoring God but was intended to invite human admiration. The reward sought was not something proper to God's realm but something worldly. This is what Jesus taught about prayer according to Matthew's Gospel:

"Take care not to practice your religion before your fellow men just to catch their eyes; otherwise, you have no reward with your Father in heaven.

"For example: when you are about to give alms, do not send a trumpeter ahead of you, as the hypocrites do in the synagogues and streets to win the applause of their fellow men. I tell you plainly, they have their reward already. When you give alms, your left hand should not know what your right is doing. Thus your alms is given in secrecy, and your Father, who sees what is secret, will reward you.

"Again, when you pray, do not be like the hypocrites, for they love to pray standing in the synagogues or at street corners to attract the attention of their fellow men. I tell you plainly, they have their reward already. When you pray, retire to your private room and bolt the door, and then pray to your Father in secrecy; and your Father, who sees what is secret, will reward you.

"Moreover, when you pray, do not use many and idle words, as the heathen do; for they think that their glibness will win them a hearing. So do not imitate them. Surely, your Father is acquainted with your needs before you ask him. The following, then, must be the pattern of your prayer:
Our Father in heaven!
May you be known and glorified,
your kingdom come,
your will be done, on earth as well as in heaven;
give us this day
our daily bread;
forgive us our debts
as we also forgive our debtors;
and do not expose us to temptation,
but deliver us from evil.
For if you forgive your fellow men their offenses, your heav-

enly Father will, in turn, forgive you; but if you do not forgive your fellow men their offenses, neither will your Father forgive your offenses.

Mt 6:1–15

The Lord's prayer

This prayer which Jesus taught is very familiar to most people in the western half of the world society. Millions of people know it "by heart," which means they have it memorized more than it means that it is united with their heart, their views about life, their feelings, or their loves.

Since we have already talked about the coming of God's kingdom, maybe you noticed when you read the "Lord's Prayer" this time that it asks for the kingdom to come. When it comes there won't be the difference there now is between what is done in heaven and what is done on earth, but God's will will rule both.

The next phrase asks for daily bread. It is especially difficult for sincere Christians to think out how Jesus' ideas on this are to be applied today. Jesus made it very clear that we human beings must trust that God will provide for daily needs. But we also know that society is so structured that unless many complex systems are enforced the goods of the world are not fairly distributed and large groups of people cannot find food, clothing or shelter. It is estimated that about ten thousand people die every day either from starvation or from the consequences of not having enough to eat. In some countries social security provides for aged people on the basis of what they earned over their lifetime. Whole businesses exist to help people provide for themselves far beyond the day. Can you think of any?

Many people provide for themselves far beyond their needs; this Jesus condemns. But what about the people who, unless they provide for themselves early, and unite in unions, or strike against industries and governments, in fact, are left destitute? We will have to search the rest of Jesus' teachings for more clues to answer these questions. We cannot doubt that Jesus meant "Give us today our daily bread." And He meant it in this sense which goes by the name of "improvident." When you say the Lord's Prayer think about where and how you stand on these issues and ask yourself how meaningful this phrase is to you. Do you live according to a psychology of trust in God? Here are more of Jesus' words on this subject:

"I tell you therefore: do not fret about what to eat, or what to drink, to sustain your life, or about what to wear on your bodies. Is not life more precious than food, and the body more precious than clothing? Look at the wild birds: they do not sow, or reap, or store up provisions in barns, and yet your heavenly Father feeds them! Are not you more precious than they? And which of you can by fretting add one minute to his span of life? And as for clothing, why do you fret? Observe the lilies in the field! How they grow! They do not toil or spin; and yet, I tell you, even Solomon in all his glory did not dress like one of these. Now if God so clothes the grass in the field, which is there today and is thrown into the furnace tomorrow, will he not much more readily clothe you? What little faith you have!

"Therefore, have done with fretting, and do not constantly be asking: 'What are we going to eat?' or, 'What are we going to drink?' or, 'What are we going to wear?' Why, the heathen make all these things an object of eager search; besides, your heavenly Father knows that you need all these things. No, let your first concern be the kingdom of God and what he requires of you; then you will have all these things thrown in for good measure. In short, have done fretting about the morrow. The morrow, surely, can do its own fretting. One evil a day is burden enough."

Mt 6:25–34

The next part of the Lord's Prayer is conditional: forgive us our debts as we forgive others. Maybe Jesus was thinking we weren't likely to handle that condition with flying colors, because after that He tells us to ask not to be tested. Forgiveness of others is a tough test. Have you ever seen accusations put in big type on the first page of a newspaper, and then some days later, by chance, found an apology for the accusation in fine print on some inner page? It happens. And of course there are plenty of other tests we might not pass, so God, hold on to us or we may get lost.

Snakes and stones

Jesus' teachings demand a real "truing up" of human relations. He tells us not to judge others and not to criticize others. In this connection He gave one of those "impossibility" stories which exaggerate His ideas beyond physical limits. These comparisons are annoying to us, since we rather inclined to be more literal, but the people in Jesus' society were less literal and not bothered by such extreme sayings as the one about a camel going through a needle's eye. Jesus said we should not try to take splinters out of our brother's eyes while ignoring the plank in our own. Then He also said we shouldn't throw pearls to pigs, and went on talking, using all sorts of fantastic contrasts. This is where the stones and the snakes come in:

> "Ask, and you will receive; seek, and you will find; knock, and you will gain admission. In fact, only he who asks receives; only he who seeks finds; only he who knocks will gain admission. Really, will anyone among you give a stone to his son that asks him for bread — or a snake, when he asks for a fish? Well, then, if you, bad as you are, choose to give useful gifts to your children, how much more will your Father in heaven give what is good to those that ask him!
>
> "In short, in all respects do to your fellowmen exactly as you wish them to do to you. This, surely, is the gist of the Law and the Prophets."

Mt 7:7–12

How do images like this one, using stones and snakes, apply to our life today? Actually there are many ways of interpreting these parables. Jesus gave an interpretation. He pointed out that we can tell good from evil so we ought not to underrate God's capacity to distinguish them or His willingness to give good things to those who ask Him.

However, it is a modern problem not to be too able to distinguish good and evil. The snakes and stones of modern life are not so obvious. For example, a negligent teacher is giving stones to seekers of bread. So is the manufacturer whose product is overpriced or falsely advertised. More hidden, but worse examples occur in the realm of politics, as when laws are made contrary to the common good, or public money is wasted, or international trade regulations are made to depress the living standards of some countries, and other things of this sort too numerous to mention. Since we can hardly recognize the snakes and stones we daily hand out to others, but still have some idea that this is what we are doing, it is not surprising we often feel far from God who is the giver of good things to those who ask for them.

Why and when to pray

The two ideas: to trust in God and to be truly honest in dealing with other men, are central to Jesus' teaching about prayer and also about behavior. Prayer life and moral or ethical life merge in the Gospels. What else can we find that is more especially about prayer? So far we have been talking about how we must be in our inner selves in order to pray, and what to say in prayer. We might ask when should we pray?

Sometimes people say "pray always," but this doesn't make too much sense; it's a bit like "eat always." Anyway when anything is always going on, like the TV in some houses, it loses meaning and soon tends to mean nothing. While Jesus was always united with His Father, God, He did not recite prayers always. It is quite clear from the Gospels that He prayed at very definite times.

Jesus prayed to prepare for the important events of His life. His prayer was tied to situations and activities. He prayed, as a sort of demonstration, before calling Lazarus to life again. He prayed after He heard of the death of John the Baptist. He prayed before doing some of His miracles. He told Peter He would pray for him so that the devil might not tempt him. One time His followers tried to cure a sick man and they did not succeed. Jesus told them that that particular case required prayer and fasting.

The best known and most dramatic examples of this prayer-to-fit-the-event in Jesus' own life are His prayer in the garden before His trial and death, His prayer at the Last Supper (mostly given in John's gospel) and His prayer before He began His public life. The description of Jesus' retreat in the desert before He began His public life is one of the most interesting in the Gospels. It teaches us much about prayer in a very graphic direct way. This is how Luke records the temptation of Jesus by the devil:

> Jesus, full of the Holy Spirit, turned away from the Jordan and was led by the Spirit into the desert to be put to the test by the devil for forty days. He did not eat anything in all that time and, when it elapsed, was hungry. The devil said to

[125]

him: "If you are God's son, command this stone to turn into a loaf of bread." But Jesus met his proposal by saying: "The Scripture says: 'Man does not live by bread alone.'" The devil also led him up to an eminence to let him see, in a flash, all the kingdoms of the inhabited world, and then said to him: "To you I am ready to give the whole extent of this vast empire and its splendor. It has been put at my disposal, and I give it to whom I please. If you, therefore, do homage to me, you shall have all of it." But Jesus countered by saying to him: "The Scripture says: 'You shall do homage to the Lord your God, and him alone shall you adore.'" Finally, he took him to Jerusalem and after setting him down upon the battlement of the temple, said to him: "If you are God's son, fling yourself down from this place. The Scripture says: 'To his angels he will give charge of you to keep your safe,' and, 'Upon their hands they will bear you up, that you may not stub your foot on a stone.'" But Jesus retorted: "The Scripture says: 'You shall not tempt the Lord your God.'" When the devil had exhausted every test, he withdrew from him till a more convenient time.

Lk 4:1–13

22. Understanding

Jesus was a teacher. But He did not explain things and then give tests, except for a few quizes to the apostles. He did not expect all the people who listened to Him to understand Him. Sometimes, when they did understand Him, Jesus said they only understood because God had helped them.

Most of the time Jesus taught by using stories in which His meaning is hidden. These stories are called parables. After retelling a number of these parables, Mark's Gospel says:

> It was by many such parables that he announced to the people the message in a manner suited to their capacity. Without parables he would not speak to them; privately, however, he interpreted everything to his immediate disciples.
>
> Mk 4:33–34

Here we see how Mark explained Jesus' teaching. Mark says Jesus' method is tied to the ability of the people to *understand* His message. Matthew says the same, bringing in another prophetic saying from Isaiah:

> "That is why I speak to them in parable style. For all their seeing they do not see, and for all their hearing they do not so hear as to understand; and thus the prophecy of Isaias is more and more fulfilled in them. It says:
> 'Your ears will hear,
> yet you will not understand;
> your eyes will look,
> yet you will not see.
> For blunted is the sense of this people:
> their ears are hard of hearing,
> and their eyes are shut;
> thus neither their eyes see,

nor their ears hear,
nor their minds understand;
and they are not converted and healed by me.'
But your eyes are blessed, for they see; and your ears are
blessed, for they hear. I tell you frankly: many prophets and
saints have longed to see what you are looking upon, yet they
did not see it, and to hear what you are listening to, yet they
did not hear it!"

Mt 13:13–17

There are two main types of knowledge. Statements such as
"David made Jerusalem his capital" inform us about facts. This is
one kind. This kind is true in a "right or wrong" sense.

The other kind of knowledge is more properly called "understanding." Our knowledge of freedom, justice, suffering, love and
the ideas which give value and meaning to life belong to this
second type of knowledge. This kind of knowledge is not right or
wrong, but it is "true" when, through it, we *see* what we recognize
as reality. The truth of understanding, (sometimes called wisdom)
goes deeper into human beings than the sensations and events
which are the information-knowledge of history and science.

Now about "understanding": it is "hot" or "cold," trivial or deep.
It has degrees and it grows in us all during our lives. Jesus asked
men and women to *understand* His message. Jesus' disciples understood Him and therefore they belonged to Him. This brings us to
the next point in our explanation.

Nowadays people think of experience, willing or deciding, feeling
knowing, and doing as if each of these aspects of life were very distinct from each other. Not Jesus. Not Isaiah. Look at the quote from
Isaiah. Isaiah made it very clear that people *will* to understand,
or they decide not to understand. When they understand they
act. They do that "turning in a new direction" which is called
conversion.

Jesus told a parable about the way men and women understand
His teachings:

"Look! The sower goes out to sow. As he sows, some of the
seed falls close to the footpath; and the birds of the air come
and eat it up. Other seed falls on stony ground, where it does
not have much soil; and, because it has no soil of any depth,

[128]

it shoots up at once; but by the time the sun has climbed the heavens, it is scorched and, because it cannot strike root, withers away. Other seed falls among the thorns, and the thorns come up and choke it. Still other seed falls on the right kind of soil, and this at last bears fruit, in some cases a hundredfold, in others sixtyfold, in yet others thirtyfold. Let everyone heed what he has heard."

Mt 13:4–9

Guess who didn't understand that parable! The disciples. Jesus explained it to them:

"For your part, then, listen to the explanation of the parable of the sower. Whenever anyone hears the message announcing the kingdom and does not really grasp it, on comes the evil one and steals what has been sown in his mind. Such a one is described by the words 'sown close to the footpath.' The words 'sown on the stony ground' describe one who, the moment he hears the message, receives it with joy; but he does not let it take root in himself; on the contrary, he is a timeserver and, when distress or persecution comes on account of the message, he is at once upset. The words 'sown among the thorns' describe one who hears the message, but the cares of this world and the deceitful attractions of wealth utterly choke the message, and it turns out barren. The words 'sown in the right kind of soil' describe one who hears and grasps the message; and he, of course, bears fruit and yields as much as a hundredfold, or sixtyfold, or thirtyfold."

Mt 13:18–23

Did you notice how hearing and doing are tied together by Jesus. There is no such thing as a disembodied mind collecting what it hears, as in an empty bucket. What goes into the ear goes into the *whole man*, and what comes out of the mouth comes out of the *whole man*. His enemies got the point of what Jesus said often better than His friends, and reacted by being offended, by wanting to stone Him to death . . . the truth hurt and they reacted like injured animals by snarling and attacking.

In the parable about good seed and a weed called darnel, Jesus said that the whole direction of a man's being is one way or another. Do not forget, when you read this parable (which makes it sound as if men are predestined to good or evil) that Jesus and John the

[129]

Baptist began their teaching by saying that the evil direction can be reversed by repentance:

> Another parable he proposed to them was this: "The kingdom of heaven reminds me of a man who has sown good seed in his field. But, while everybody is asleep, his enemy comes and sows weeds among the wheat, and goes away. Eventually the blades spring up and put forth heads, but by that time the weeds also crop out. So the help of the landowner approach him and say: 'Sir, was it not good seed that you sowed in your field? How, then, is it overrun with weeds?' 'That is the work of an enemy!' he replies. 'Well,' say the help to him, 'do you want us to go and gather them up?' 'Not at all,' he answers; 'otherwise, in gathering the weeds, you might pull up the wheat along with them. Let both grow until the harvest, and, when harvest time has come, I will say to the reapers: 'Gather up, first of all, the weeds and bind them in bundles to be burnt; after that, store the wheat in my barn.'"

> He then left the crowds and went indoors. Here the disciples interviewed him. "Explain to us," they said, "the parable of the weeds in the field." And this was his answer: "The sower of the good seed is the Son of Man. The field is the world. The good seed are the born citizens of the realm. The weeds are the brood of the wicked one. The enemy who planted them is the devil. The harvest time is the end of the world. The reapers are the angels. Just as the weeds, therefore, are gathered in bundles and burnt, so it will be at the end of the world: the Son of Man will send his angels, and they will weed his kingdom of all seducers and evildoers, and hurl them into the fiery furnace. There it is that weeping and gnashing of teeth will really be heard. Then the saints will shine like the sun in the kingdom of their Father. Let everyone heed what he has heard.

Mt 13:24–30, 36–43

The test of understanding

As far as Jesus is concerned, the "test" of how well His lessons are understood comes in the living of daily life. Quizzes about Jesus' teachings are always surprises. They are happenings which turn up on the Pennsylvania Turnpike, Highway 101, or the Strand. They turn up in slums, in the suburbs and on the prairie, in the kitchen, the supermarket, the factory, on the docks and in the office. Jesus set His story on the road to Jericho. Remember that Levites were members of the privileged priestly class in Israel and that the Samaritans were social outcasts:

> Presently an expert in the Law came forward to sound him out. "Rabbi," he said, "what must I do to obtain a place in eternal life?" "Well," he replied, "what does the Law say about it? What do you read in it?" He answered: " 'Love the Lord your God with your whole heart, and with your whole soul, and with your whole strength, and with your whole mind'; and besides, 'Love your neighbor as yourself.' " "Your answer is correct," he said to him: "act accordingly, and you will have life." But, being anxious to justify his question, the man said to Jesus, "And whom, pray, must I consider a neighbor?"
>
> Jesus complied with his request and said: "Once upon a time, a man who was on his way from Jerusalem down to Jericho fell in with bandits; they stripped and beat him, and then went their way, leaving him half dead. By some chance a priest was going down the same road; but when he saw the man, he made a detour. In like manner a levite came near the spot and he, too, made a detour at sign of him. Finally a Samaritan came near him, and he, on seeing the man, was stirred to pity. He went up to him and bound up his wounds, pouring wine and oil into them. He then mounted him on his own beast of burden and brought him to an inn, where he took care of him. Moreover, on the morrow he produced two denarii to pay the innkeeper, and left these instructions: 'Take good care of him; and in case you spend anything over and above this sum, I will repay you on my way back.' Now which of these three men seems to you to have taken a neighborly interest in the man who had fallen in with bandits?" "The one," he replied, "who pitied him in that practical way." "Very well, then," Jesus said to him, "model your conduct on his."

Lk 10:25–37

The parable of the good Samaritan shows how men respond to situations out of their whole inner selves. The Samaritan found a way to help the injured man. Better put, he invented a way. He

[131]

had no "guide Book for Good Samaritans" to thumb through for the right formula. Apparently he could not abandon his business trip to care for the man, but he was creative enough to do something positive with the means and the limitations he had. This is real understanding: the making of reality to correspond with an idea (here love of neighbor) by doing something original and effective.

We started this chapter with an analysis of knowledge. Now let's think about the parable of the good Samaritan this way. This story Jesus told has led millions of people to see, to understand, and to make love-of-others a part of themselves. This is teaching "for real." True ideas are to moral and spiritual life like food to physical life, the necessary support to activity. If we get this idea we can read the Bible without the silly questions which are so common, such as, do you believe in the Bible?

How to live truthfully

The parable of the good Samaritan is about a short-term situation. Did Jesus give any clues to help us make the long-term creative decisions of our lives? Did he say anything that might help us to decide whether to be tinkers or tailors? Nowadays we all (both girls and boys) have to decide for ourselves what works and studies to pursue in life, what political position to support, and whether, when and whom to marry. For most of our ancestors these things were decided by their society or family.

Jesus *did* tell us quite a bit that's useful to help us decide and to make our whole life be based on an understanding of God's hopes for mankind. One thing he told us is to not be preoccupied with making money or impressing other people. What a relief to be rid of these two burdens. He told it pretty rough and straight: if we choose to follow Him, which means to direct our lives toward God, we may have to break with our families and friends. The idea of charity, or love, teaches us not to do this unless we have to, but when we have to, we have to, for the sake of truth and justice and with no regrets or guilt feelings. In the past this has been applied mostly to people who wanted to lead lives dedicated to religion, but there is nothing in the Bible to suggest it was meant so narrowly. It applies to anyone who chooses to work for a more perfect society in a way that parents or friends oppose. Some young people have to break with their parents simply because they don't "buy" the idea of piling up wealth. Other people have to make a hard choice between old friends and the need to oppose race prejudice.

There is a story told in the Synoptic Gospels about a young man who wanted to live right. The story has been interpreted as a recommendation for the special religious life, and it is. However, the story does not imply that the special religious life is higher than other lives or meant for everyone. It was simply the advice Jesus gave this particular man. In the first part of the story Jesus found out, by questioning him, where he already stood. Then from where he had already arrived, good enough so that Jesus could look at him with love, the special religious life was what he lacked, and the rejection of wealth was the conversion he could not accept:

As he was leaving the house to pursue his journey, someone ran up and, kneeling before him, asked this question: "Good Rabbi, what must I do to inherit eternal life?" "Why do you call me good?" Jesus replied: "Nobody is good except One alone — God! You know the commandments: Do not murder; do not commit adultery; do not steal; do not bear false witness; do not commit fraud; honor your father and mother." "Rabbi," he said to him, "I have guarded against all these things from my youth." Jesus looked at him intently and loved him. Then he said to him: "One thing is still wanting to you: go, sell all you have and give the proceeds to the poor, and you will have an investment in heaven; then come back and be my follower." But he frowned at the words and went away with a heavy heart; for he had much property.

Then, looking round, Jesus said to his disciples: "Oh, with what difficulty will those who have the goods of this world enter the kingdom of God!" The disciples were dumfounded at his words. But Jesus took occasion to repeat his statement: "Children, how difficult it is for those who put their trust in worldly goods to enter the kingdom of God! It is easier for a camel to pass through the eye of a needle than for a rich man to enter the kingdom of God!" They were completely bewildered and said to one another: "In that case, who can be saved?" Jesus looked straight at them and said: "Where man fails, God still avails. God can do all things."

Mk 10:17–31

There was one poor fellow whom Jesus cured of insanity. He wanted to stay with Jesus, but Jesus told him his vocation was to return to his home to spread the Good News there:

> The man, however, out of whom the demons had been driven, asked leave to stay with him; but he sent him away with the remark: "Go back home, and explain all that God has done for you." So he went away and published all over town what Jesus had done for him.
>
> Lk 8:38–39

Later, in the letters written by Paul, we find the idea that there are many different gifts or vocations given by God. And we should pursue them energetically. What is of over-all importance is not the special work or vocation, but the charity which is in them all and above them all:

> You are Christ's body and individually its members. And God has established in his Church some in the first rank, namely apostles, others in the second rank, namely inspired preachers, and still others in the third rank, namely teachers. After that come wonder-workers, then those with the gifts of healing, then assistants, administrators, and those that speak a variety of languages.
>
> Are all of us apostles? Are all of us inspired preachers? Are all of us teachers? Are all of us wonder-workers? Do all of us have the gifts of healing? Do all of us speak in languages? Do all of us act as interpreters?
>
> Be eager always to have the gift that is more precious than all the others. I am now going to point out to you the way by far the most excellent.
>
> If I should speak the languages of men and of angels, but have no love, I am no more than a noisy gong and a clanging cymbal. And if I should have the gift of inspired utterance, and have the key to all secrets, and master the whole range of knowledge, and if I should have wonder-working confidence so as to be able to move mountains, but have no love, I am nothing. And if I should distribute all I have bit by bit, and should yield my body to the flames, but have no love, it profits me nothing.
>
> Love is long-suffering; love is kind, and is not envious; love does not brag; it is not conceited; it is not ill-mannered; it is

[134]

not self-seeking; it is not irritable, it takes no note of injury; it is not glad when injustice triumphs; it is glad when the truth prevails. Always it is ready to make allowances; always to trust; always to hope; always to be patient.

Love will never end. If there are inspired utterances, they will become useless. If there are languages, they will be discarded. If there is knowledge, it will become useless. For our knowledge is incomplete, and our utterances inspired by God are incomplete, but when that which is perfect has come, what is incomplete will be useless.

1 Cor 12:27–13:10

The gospel parable of the "talents" is probably the main vocation story of those attributed to Jesus. In this story three men are each given talents — a sum of money — to trade with. The amount each man is given is proportionate to his ability. The two given larger amounts each double their original money. It is the fellow with the least ability who saves his, does not take any risk and does not have his money grow. The first two are rewarded and the third is punished.

There is another parable that seems to tell the opposite message: this is the parable about the vineyard workers. In this case some men are employed from the labor pool in the market place early in the morning, and others later in the day. Toward the end of the day there are still some men left in the market place unemployed. The owner of the vineyard calls them also. But when it comes time to pay all these workers, although some have worked longer and harder than others, the owner gives them all the same pay. Those who had worked the longest then complain and ask for more pay. Their request is refused.

Like all parables, this one can be interpreted in various ways. But if we remember from the parable about the talents that each man realized a profit proportionate to his ability, then the stories are not dissimilar. In each story the men who were rewarded did what they were able to do: it was not the fault of the social-rejects hired at the eleventh hour that they did less than their readily employed co-workers.

Taken together these stories tell us to take risks and do what we can, trusting that God, who knows us and our circumstances, will reward us. Jesus never declared that men were equally gifted or equally rewarded. He did make clear that whatever gift we have, no matter how little, must be risked in use: the whole growth of the whole person in response to truth is all (the least) and the all (the most) He asks of us. And if, like the prodigal son, we make a total mess of everything, so long as we have not lost our understanding of love, our Heavenly Father will welcome us home.

23. Living Parables

Toward the end of the Bible there are some short letters. In one of these, called the First Letter of John, the writer asks how the children of God and the children of the devil or evil can be distinguished from each other. Then he answers his own question by saying that love is the mark by which the friend of God is recognized:

> Here is the sign which reveals who are God's children and who are the devil's: Whoever fails to lead a holy life is no child of God, neither is he who fails to love his brother.
>
> This is precisely the message which you have heard from the beginning — that we should love one another. Be not like Cain who was a child of the evil one and murdered his brother. Why did he murder him? Because his own life was wicked, whereas his brother's was holy. Do not be surprised, brothers, if the world hates you. We know that we have passed from death to life, because we love our brothers. He who does not love abides in death. Everyone who hates his brother is a murderer, and you know that no murderer has eternal life abiding in him.
>
> We know what love is from the fact that Jesus Christ laid down his life for us. We, too, ought to lay down our lives for our brothers. How, then, can the love of God abide in him who possesses worldly goods, and, seeing his brother in need, closes his heart to him? Little children, let us not love merely in word or with the tongue, but in action, in reality.
>
> 1 Jn 3:10–18

During His life Jesus gave many examples of real and active love to His followers. Or, and it would be more accurate to say this, He

[137]

analysed situations for them so they could recognize the love and lack of love which was present. Jesus often had to point out the absurdity of the Sabbath regulations the Hebrews of His time thought to be a way of honoring God. He kept telling them that God was not pleased with any ritual formality which actually prevented charitable activity.

Such an idea tends to develop among religious people. Maybe this is one reason Jesus brought it up so often. It can also be seen as a warning about institutional religion and its relation to love. Isn't it paradoxical that the defenders of religion among the Hebrews, were those who wanted to kill, that is, to commit a crime against the commandments they supposedly upheld? Jesus mentioned that the institutional religious leaders were responsible for the killing of the prophets. He was fully aware of their desire to kill Him. They decided to expel from the house of worship anyone who might suggest that Jesus was the long waited Messiah. This is mentioned in the strange cross-examination of the man born blind. We'll come to that story later in this chapter. Here are two biblical passages which illustrate this perverse but all too human reaction of the religious leaders to Jesus' miracles of curing:

> The following occurred on another Sabbath. He went to the synagogue to teach, and a man whose right arm was withered was present. The Scribes and the Pharisees were closely watching him, to see whether he would heal on the Sabbath. They wanted to find grounds for accusing him. He was well aware of their thoughts; so he said to the man with the withered arm: "Rise, and come forward." He rose and came forward. Jesus then said to them: "I ask you: is it 'right' on the Sabbath to do an act of kindness, or must one inflict evil? to save a life, or must one kill?" Then, glancing round at them all, he said to the man, "Stretch out your arm." He did so, and his arm was fully restored. But they brimmed over with fury. . . .
> Lk 6:6–11

Refining the ability to see oneself

The absurdity of the Jewish sabbath regulations is obvious enough to us, but it was not so obvious to the people in Jesus' time, even His friends. When He died they did not think of going near his tomb, or of caring for His dead body, until the sabbath was over.

LUKE

The same Luke who wrote one of the four Gospels also wrote a book about what happened just after Jesus' death. This book is called "The Acts of the Apostles," or "Acts" for short. It is one of the few biblical texts whose authorship has never been disputed. It continues the Gospel Luke wrote and probably was not separated from it until 150 A.D.

In the book of Acts Luke tells us about two main series of activities: the formation of the first Christian communities and the missionary journeys made by Paul. The texts themselves tell what is known about Luke. He may have been a Hebrew who knew Greek well, or else he was a Greek who knew a lot about Jewish affairs. He seems to have known something about medicine. He traveled with Paul; they were together at least five years. Luke does not mention anything which happened later than 70 A.D.

The works of Luke are careful compilations from different sources plus his own account of what he actually saw. When he was present at an event he wrote about it in the first person, "we" did such and such. Otherwise he used "they" or "he." His language also varies. He tried to translate non-Greek sources so exactly that he put them in poor Greek and wrote better Greek when he told about his own experiences. He knew, personally, many of the people he tells about, especially Paul and the deacon Philip.

There are stories in the Bible which show how Jesus probed beneath superficially nice people to expose their smallness and lack of love. Here are two of these stories.

It makes the first a little clearer to know that it was a customary courtesy in Jesus' society for a slave to wash the feet of guests when they arrived at a private home. Also, when people ate formally they reclined on couches, on their sides, with their heads nearest the table and their feet away from it.

One day, one of the Pharisees invited him to a meal with him. He entered the home of the Pharisee and reclined on a couch; and without warning a woman who was a scandal in the town came in. After making sure that he was at table in the home of the Pharisee, she brought with her an alabaster flask of perfume, took her stand behind him at his feet, and wept. Yielding to an impulse, she rained her tears on his feet and wiped them with her hair; she tenderly kissed his feet and anointed them with the perfume. His host, the Pharisee, noticed this, and said to himself: "This man, if he were a prophet, would know who and what sort of creature this woman is, that make so much fuss over him! Why, she is a scandalous person!"

Jesus read his thoughts and said to him: "Simon, I have something to tell you." "Tell it, Rabbi," he replied. "Once upon a time two men were in the debt of a moneylender. The one owed him five hundred denarii; the other, fifty. Neither of them was in a position to pay; so he made both of them happy by canceling their debts. Under these circumstances, which of them will be more generous in loving him?" "The one, I suppose," answered Simon, "whom he made happy by canceling the greater amount." "Your judgment is correct," he replied. Then, turning to the woman, he said to Simon: "Do you see this woman? I came into your house, and you offered me no water for my feet: but this woman rained her tears upon my feet and wiped them dry with her hair. You gave me no kiss of welcome; but this woman has not left off, from the time I entered, tenderly kissing my feet. You did not anoint my head with oil: but this woman anointed my feet with perfume. And in consideration of this I tell you: her sins, numerous as they are, are forgiven. You see, she has shown so much love! One, of course, who has but little forgiven him, shows but little love." He then said to her: "Your sins are forgiven." At once his fellow guests gave way to thoughts like this: "Who is this individual who even forgives sins!" He finally said to the woman: "Your faith has saved you. Go home and be at peace."

Lk 7:35–50

The second of these two stories isn't even about love: it's about ordinary justice. These sanctimonious fakers had apparently forgotten, among other things, that the law of Moses said that, in the case of adultery, both the man and the woman were to be punished.

In the morning he again appeared in the temple, where the people flocked to him in crowds; and he sat down to teach them. Here the Scribes and the Pharisees brought a woman caught in adultery and, placing her in view of all, said to him: "Rabbi, this woman has been caught in the act of committing adultery. Now in the Law, Moses has commanded us to stone women of this kind. What, then, do you say?" They said this to set a trap for him, to have matter for accusing him. But Jesus bent down and with his finger drew figures on the ground. They persisted, however, in questioning him; so he raised his head and said to them: "If there is one among you free from sin, let him be the first to throw a stone at her." Then, bending down again, he continued drawing figures on the ground; but, on hearing this, they stole away, one by one, beginning with the older men, till he was left alone with the woman still standing in full view. Jesus then raised his head and said to her: "Madame, where are they? Has no one condemned you?" "No one, sir," she replied. Then Jesus said to her: "Neither do I condemn you. Go, and from now on sin no more."

Jn 8:2–11

The cure of the man born blind

Jesus cured many, many people. Only a few of these cures are described in the Bible; most are simply mentioned in general phrases such as "he cured them." Some of the cures which are described are illustrations of particular ideas, such as this one, which is a short sermon on gratitude:

The following occurred on his pilgrimage to Jerusalem, as he passed along the borders of Samaria and Galilee. He was about to enter a village when ten lepers came his way. They

[141]

stopped at some distance, and with raised voices cried out: "Rabbi Jesus, take pity on us." Noticing them, he said: "Go, and get yourselves examined by the priests." And this is what happened: while still on their way, they were made clean. Now one of them, seeing that he was cured, turned back, loudly praising God; he threw himself on his face at Jesus' feet and thanked him. And this was a Samaritan! "Were not the ten made clean?" Jesus asked; "Where are the other nine? Oh to find that not one has returned to give glory to God except this foreigner!" He then said to him: "You may rise and go home. Your faith has cured you."

Lk 17:11–19

One further point about prayer which Jesus talked about (although we didn't mention it in our brief chapter) was perseverance. Jesus told a story about an unjust judge who was pushed by a widow to treat her justly. She pestered him into it. Then there was man who didn't want to answer his door during the night, but he finally did because his friend wouldn't stop knocking. There are many short stories with this theme. Here is the story of a miracle which would not have happened but for perseverance:

One day about that time he was engaged in teaching. In the audience there were Pharisees and teachers of the Law, who had come from every village in Galilee and Judea, including Jerusalem; and the Lord's power was active, enabling him to cure. Here a strange thing happened: a group of men, carrying upon a mat a man who was paralyzed, endeavored to bring him in and set him down in front of him; but owing to the crowd, they found no way of edging him in; so they went up to the roof and, through a hole in the tiles, let him down, mat and all, right under the eyes of Jesus. When he saw their faith, he said: "My good man, your sins are now forgiven." The Scribes and the Pharisees assumed a critical attitude. "Who is this man," they said, "who utters blasphemies? Who has power to forgive sins except God alone?" Aware of their criticism, Jesus reasoned with them as follows: "Why are you in such a critical mood? Which is easier, to say, 'Your sins are now forgiven,' or to say, 'Rise, and be on your feet again'? But I want you to understand that the Son of Man has power to forgive sins on earth." He then addressed the paralyzed man:

[142]

"I command you: rise, take up your mat, and go home." Immediately the man rose in the presence of all, took up the mat he had been lying on, and went home glorifying God.

Lk 5:17–25

But of all the stories of cures — not of the raising of people from the dead which have another level of power and significance — of all the stories of cures the story of the blind beggar is the most real and complete. The description of Jesus is very detailed. Lots of people are portrayed, most of them behaving with normal human mixes of brilliance and stupidity. The whole story is delightful. Here it is, from the Gospel of John:

One day he saw, in passing, a man blind from birth. So his disciples asked him: "Rabbi, who has sinned, this man or his parents, to account for his being born blind?" "Neither this man has sinned," replied Jesus, "nor his parents. No. God simply wants to make use of him to reveal his ways. Our duty is, while it is day, to conform to the ways of him whose ambassador I am. Night is coming on, when no man can do anything. As long as I am in the world, I am the light of the world." With these words spoken, he spat on the ground, and by means of the spittle made a lump of mud, and then spread the mud over his eyes, and said to him: "Go, and wash in the pool of Siloam" — a word which in our language means "Ambassador." So he went, and washed, and came back able to see.

Now the neighbors and the people who had seen him before — for he was a beggar — said: "Is not this the fellow who used to sit and beg in such and such a place?" Some said: "This is the man." Others said: "Not at all; he only looks like him." He himself declared: "I am the man." They asked him therefore: "How, then, were your eyes opened?" "The man called Jesus," he replied, "made a lump of mud and spread it over my eyes and said to me: 'Go to Siloam and wash.' So I went and washed, and got my sight." When they asked him: "Where is this man?" he replied: "I do not know."

The man who had been blind was then taken before the Pharisees. Now it happened that the day on which Jesus had formed the lump of mud and opened his eyes was a Sabbath. So the Pharisees, for their part, asked him how he had obtained sight. He replied: "He put a lump of mud on my eyes, and I washed, and now I see."

[143]

Then some of the Pharisees said: "That man has no authority from God; he does not observe the Sabbath." Others argued: "How can a sinner give such proofs of power!" As a result, there was disagreement among them. So they asked the blind man again: "What do you say about him, because he opened your eyes?" He answered: "He is a prophet."

The Jews, therefore, did not believe that he had been blind and then obtained sight, until they summoned the parents of the man himself who had regained his sight, and put this question to them: "Is this your son? And do you say he was born blind? How, then, is he at present able to see?" His parents gave this explanation: "We know that this is our son, and that he was born blind; but how he is now able to see we do not know, nor do we know who opened his eyes. Ask him himself; he is old enough; he will give his own account." His parents said this because they were afraid of the Jews; for the Jews had already agreed among themselves that, if anyone should acknowledge Christ as the Messias, he should be put out of the synagogue. That was why his parents said: "He is old enough; ask him himself."

So they summoned a second time the man who had been blind, and said to him: "Give glory to God! We know that this man is a sinner." "Whether or not he is a sinner I do not know," he replied; "one thing I do know: I was blind and now I see." Then they asked him: "What did he do to you? How did he open your eyes?" "I told you already," he replied, "and you did not take my word for it. Why do you want to hear it again? Do you, too, perhaps, want to become his disciples?" Then they heaped abuse on him. "You are a disciple of that man," they said; "we are disciples of Moses. We know that Moses is God's spokesman, but whose mouthpiece this man is we do not know." "Why," the man retorted, "the strange thing is that you do not know whose mouthpiece he is when, as a matter of fact, he has opened my eyes! We know that God does not listen to sinners; but when one is God-fearing and does his will, he does listen to him. Since the world began, it is unheard of that anyone opened the eyes of one born blind! If this man had no mission from God, he could do nothing!" By way of answer they said to him: "You were wholly born in sin, and you mean to teach us?" And they expelled him.

Jesus was informed that they had expelled him. When he

met the man, he said: "Do you believe in the Son of God?" "Well, who is he, sir?" the man answered; "I want to believe in him." "You are now looking in his face," replied Jesus; "yes, it is he who is now speaking to you!" "I do believe, sir," he said; and he fell on his knees before him.

Jn 9:1–38

Did you notice how this beggar grew steadily and his understanding of God increased. First he knew no more about Jesus than His name. Then he realized, from his own argument, that Jesus was a prophet who truly came from God. Finally he recognized Jesus as the Son of Man, whom he hoped to meet. He worshipped Jesus. The story helps us to grow to understand what sin is: physical blindness does not cause sin but spiritual blindness is caused by sin.

24. The Gift of Life

Jesus brought new life to men and women. He didn't just bring an after-life. It is true that God wills to fulfill the promise which we know from our experience of being alive (the goodness of life and its incompleteness here on earth), and that Jesus' death and His message have an importance with respect to eternal life, but this is not the whole "Good News."

Jesus did not start eternal life. The men and women who lived before He came on earth weren't left out. As Jesus said, God is a God of the living — the living Jacob and Isaac and David. Jesus told one parable in which Abraham is pictured with God, and several other times He made it clear that there was no "before" and "after" His own death with respect to human virtue and its eternal reward. There were many good men and bad before Jesus came, and there have been good men and bad since. Jesus described good and bad men as active people doing what their inner reality led them to do:

> "For as no healthy tree bears sickly fruit, so, no sickly tree bears healthy fruit. In fact, each tree is known by its distinctive fruit. Surely, figs are not picked from thornbushes, nor are grapes harvested from thistles."

Lk 6:43–45

Jesus emphasized the activity:

> "Why do you address me 'Master, Master,' when you do not do what I say? When anyone comes to me who listens to my teaching and acts accordingly — let me show you whom such a one is like: he is like a man who carefully builds a house; he digs deep into the ground and lays a foundation upon rock;

[146]

and, in case a flood comes, the torrent may beat against that house, but is unable to shake it off its base, for it has been solidly built. But he who just listens and does not act accordingly is like a man who hastily builds a house upon the bare ground without a foundation: the torrent beats against that house, and it immediately collapses and is reduced to a mighty heap of ruins."

Lk 6:46–49

Nonetheless, Jesus' coming made a difference. Jesus did ask men to have faith in Him to some purpose. Paul described the difference once as a "coming-of-age" of mankind. Paul pictured the chosen people as living in the childhood of God's heir, under the discipline proper to minors. With Jesus' coming the freedom of adult life began — adulthood in which we meet God as a brother and friend as well as a father. As adults the sons now have personal control of the riches their father always intended for them. This throws some light on the puzzling question: what difference did Jesus' life make in human life and human history?

In this brief work I am not going to answer this question. My reason is partly that I don't know the whole answer and partly because this question has to be answered personally. To answer it is to "put on the new man" and "live in Christ," as Paul said. I have some ideas about my personal answer and the direction it is taking, but that is my life's story, not yours. You have to find yours.

I do want to make two suggestions. One is that living by Jesus' teachings does make this life, here and now, more abundant, freer and happier. This doesn't mean that affluence is proof of virtue, but that what Jesus taught us helps us to rejoice in the goodness of life and to seek its goods for our neighbors. We should rejoice in our neighbor's happiness, and also sorrow when he is deprived — as Jesus said in the sermon on the mountain, mourn with those that mourn. Adapting this idea to the present, we can see that we are called to share in the sorrow of the miserable of the earth. Jesus does not want us to reject life, or reject other people. When so-called followers of Jesus have claimed "we alone are saved" and have persecuted or imposed restrictions on others they have not been following Jesus. Most asceticism (self-discipline cultism) is perverse egoism, as is shown by its fruits. Jesus meant self-discipline to be the by-product of situations. Self-discipline is needed at times so that growth and activity may be more effective.

The other point is that, although Jesus did mention rewards, He didn't make rewards into a motivation system. We are not meant to do good out of self-interest in being rewarded, but because goodness is reality. If we set out to become what we are and grow in the ways in which we are images of God, being united with Him someday won't be such a shock that we have to gear all our life here to meeting it. Let's live as if the kingdom has come, here and now. Because it has. The good world God created is not alien to God. To perfect this world is the work He gave mankind to do here.

Bread in the wilderness

Jesus said "I am the bread of life," and He illustrated this idea by providing large groups of people with bread. These miracles illustrate the theme that God will provide daily bread for those who abandon themselves to Him, but then Jesus had to caution the people against being too interested in this material provision. He told them to take it in stride, keeping God first.

Here is the report of one of these miracles. In this description Jesus makes a suggestion to His followers. See if you find it. This text is from Luke's Gospel, the Gospel in which the sequence of events seems sometimes to be important. So remember that the twelve had just returned from a missionary journey:

> The apostles finally returned and told him in detail what success they had had. He then took them with him and, for the sake of privacy, withdrew in the direction of a town called Bethsaida. The crowds came to know about it and followed him. He received them kindly, spoke to them about the kingdom of God, and cured those in need of attention.
>
> The day was now well on its way to decline. So the Twelve approached and said to him: "Dismiss the crowd so that they can reach the villages and farms round about, and find lodging and provisions. Here we are in a lonely place." But he replied: "It is for you to give them something to eat." "We do not have more than five loaves and two fish," they said, "unless we go ourselves and buy food for this whole crowd." There were, in fact, about five thousand men present. He then said to his disciples: "Have them recline in groups of about fifty

persons each." They did so, and had them all recline. Then
he took the five loaves and the two fish into his hands, and,
looking up to heaven, said grace over them, and broke them
into portions which he gave to the disciples to serve to the
crowd. All ate, and everyone had a plentiful meal. Besides,
what was left over from their meal was gathered up, in all
twelve baskets of remnants.

Lk 9:10–17

Water of life

Jesus sometimes bewildered His apostles. We can see this in a
story retold by John so vividly that it seems to have been an experience he lived over and over all his life. It is realistically retold:
take the last remark of the converted Samaritans: instead of saying "thank you" to the woman who was Jesus' first messenger, they
tell her off. Isn't that just like people? And the apostles who went
to get Jesus food seem peeved when after all their loving effort to
do something for Him, He passes up what they gave Him. Notice
also how the woman grew from recognizing Jesus as a prophet to
announcing him as the savior. These are side aspects of the story,
however. The main point is its revelation of Jesus' teaching and
mission:

Now word had come to the Pharisees that Jesus was gaining
and baptizing more disciples than John. Jesus was aware of
this, and therefore — though, really, it was not Jesus that did
the baptizing, but his disciples — he quit Judea and went back
again to Galilee. Since he had to pass through Samaria, he
came to a Samaritan town called Sychar near the place which
Jacob had given to his son Joseph. Jacob's well was there;
and so, since he was fatigued from journeying on foot, he
simply sat down by the well. It was about noon.

Now there came a Samaritan woman to draw water. "Let
me have a drink," Jesus said to her. His disciples had gone
off to town to buy provisions. "How can you, a Jew," the Samaritan woman said to him, "ask me, a Samaritan woman, for
a drink?" The fact is, Jews have no dealings with Samaritans.
Jesus answered her: "If you understood God's gift and knew
who he is that said to you, 'Let me have a drink,' you would
have asked him, and he would have given you living water."
"Sir," the woman replied, "you have no bucket, and the well

[149]

is deep. Where, then, do you get the living water? Are you greater than our father Jacob, who gave us the well out of which he and his children and his flocks used to drink?" "Anyone," replied Jesus, "who drinks of this water will thirst again; but he who drinks of the water which I will give him will never thirst. No, the water which I will give him will become in him a fountain of water welling up into eternal life." "Sir," replied the woman, "let me have the water you speak of. I do not want to keep on getting thirsty and making this trip to draw water."

"Go," he then said to her, "call your husband and come back here." "I have no husband," the woman frankly admitted. "You were right," Jesus said to her, "when you said you had no husband. You had five husbands, and the man with whom you are now living is not your husband. What you said is perfectly true."

"I see, sir," the woman said to him, "you are a prophet! Our fathers worshiped on this mountain, and your people say that Jerusalem is the place for worshiping." "Take my word for it, madam," Jesus replied, "a time is coming when you will worship the Father neither on this mountain nor in Jerusalem. You worship what you do not know; we worship what we do know. Salvation comes from the Jews. And yet a time is coming, in fact, it is now here, when true worshipers will worship the Father in spirit and in truth. Such are the worshipers the Father demands. God is Spirit, and his worshipers must worship in spirit and in truth." "I know very well," the woman said, "that the Messias" — the Christ, as he is called — "is to come and, when he comes, will tell us everything." Jesus then said to her: "I am he — I who now speak to you."

At this point the disciples returned and were surprised to find him conversing with a woman; but no one asked: "What do you want?" or, "Why did you talk to her?" The woman then left her pitcher behind and went into town. "Come and see a man," she said to the inhabitants, "who told me everything I ever did! Can he, perhaps, be the Messias?" And some actually stirred out of town and came to meet him.

Meanwhile his disciples were pleading with him: "Rabbi, eat, please." Jesus replied: "I have a food to eat of which you are ignorant." Then the disciples said among themselves: "Did someone, perhaps, bring him something to eat?" Jesus said to them: "To do the will of him whose ambassador I am, and to complete the work he has assigned — that is my food! Would you not say, 'Four months yet — then is the time for harvesting'? Now mark what I tell you: raise your eyes and look at the fields! Already they are white and ripe for the harvest! The reaper is getting wages and gathering fruit for eternal life, so that planter and reaper may rejoice together; for in this case the saying, 'One does the planting, and another the reaping,' is to the point. I am sending you to reap a field in which you have not toiled; others have done the toiling, and to the fruits of their toil you have fallen heirs."

Many of the inhabitants of that Samaritan town believed in him because the woman testified that he had told her everything she had done. So when the Samaritans met him, they pressed him to stay with them; and he did stay there two days. As a result, many more believed in him thanks to his preaching; and then they would say to the woman: "Now we no longer believe on account of your story. We have heard for ourselves and are convinced that this is indeed the Savior of the world."

Jn 4:1–42

Jesus' power over life

Jesus did not raise many dead people to life again. He did not come to end natural death. The people He brought back to life died again later like everyone else does. Jesus also died. The Gospels suggest motives for each of the times when Jesus did bring people back to mortal life. Of course, these acts were important as signs of Jesus' power.

In the three Synoptic Gospels' re-telling of the raising of Jairus' daughter a second miracle is sandwiched in between the two halves of the story. In this other miracle Jesus speaks of feeling power going from Himself to a woman in the crowd. Here is Luke's text:

When Jesus returned, the crowd welcomed him; for they had all been waiting for him. Presently, there came a man whose name was Jairus, an official of the synagogue. Throwing himself down at the feet of Jesus, he implored him to come to his house; for he had an only daughter, twelve years of age, who was at the point of death. And he made his way to the place, the crowds all but smothered him.

[151]

Meanwhile, a woman who had had hemorrhages for twelve years, and had spent all her means of sustenance on physicians, but could not be cured by anyone, approached from behind and touched the fringe of his cloak. Her hemorrhage stopped immediately. "Who has touched me?" Jesus asked. But all denied having done so, and Peter remarked: "Why, Master, the crowds are pressing round you and all but crush you!" But Jesus said: "Someone has touched me. I was aware that my healing power had been at work." When the woman realized that she had not escaped notice, she came tremblingly forward and, throwing herself down before him, told, in the hearing of all the people, her reason for touching him, and how she had been instantly cured. He then said to her: "My daughter, your faith has cured you. Go home and be at peace."

He was still speaking, when a messenger from the household of the synagogue official arrived to say: "Your daughter is dead. Do not trouble the Rabbi any further." But Jesus, on hearing the message, reassured him: "You have nothing to fear. Only have faith, and she will be safe." Arrived at the home, he did not allow anyone to enter with him except Peter, James, and John, besides the child's father and mother. Everyone was weeping and lamenting her. But he said: "Stop crying; she is not dead; she is asleep." They laughed at him, knowing that she was dead. But he took her by the hand and said in a loud voice: "My child, awake." Her spirit returned, and she rose immediately. He then ordered that something to eat should be given to her. Her parents were beside themselves with wonder; but he enjoined them not to tell anyone what had taken place.

Lk 8:40–56

In the case of the dead young man at the town of Naim, Jesus seems to have been moved by concern for the man's mother. A widow without children could be in very desperate straights in Hebrew society:

Shortly afterwards he set out for a town called Naim. His disciples and a great crowd accompanied him. Just when he came near the gate of the town, a dead man — his mother's only son — was being carried out for burial. This woman was a widow, and a considerable number of townspeople were with her. The sight of her touched the Lord's heart, and he said

[152]

JOHN

There are several biblical writings said to be by John who was one of Jesus' apostles. He was the son of Zebedee and brother of the apostle James. These writings are the Fourth Gospel, the book of Revelations, and three short letters. Because the language in some of these works is so different from the language in others, scholars are sure they were not all written by the same person. It is possible that the same person dictated them to different followers who wrote them down, or that they are notes taken by John's followers. However these books and letters were written, the apostle John seems to have been their source of information. They are full of intimate details no others would have known and have similarities in thought, or themes that John seems to have thought about all the time.

For a while some scripture scholars dated John's Gospel late in the second century. Now more ancient manuscripts have been found which show that these scholars were wrong. The belief held down the centuries, that the gospel at least was put into the form in which we have it by John's disciples at about the time John died may be the true one. John died about 100 A.D.

to her: "Do not weep." He then went up to the coffin and laid his hand on it. The bearers stopped, and he said: "Young man, I command you, awake!" The dead man sat up and began to speak. He then restored him to his mother. A feeling of awe came over all, and they praised God. "A mighty prophet has risen among us!" they commented, and, "God has visited his people!" This talk about him spread throughout the Jewish land and the whole adjacent country.

Lk 7:11–17

Lazarus, come out!

Jesus brought one of His close friends back to life. This miracle was done near Jerusalem, and toward the end of Jesus' public life when His relations with various groups had pretty much crystalized. His enemies had firmly decided against Him. His apostles had matured in their understanding of His teachings about as much as they seemed able to before the coming of the Spirit. They had made up their minds about their relationships with Jesus.

Since John tells us what happened and then explains the reactions of the Jewish leaders, you can easily see for yourself what this miracle meant to different people:

Now a man named Lazarus was ill. He was of Bethany, the village where Mary and her sister Martha were living. Mary is the person who anointed the Lord with perfume and wiped his feet with her hair. It was her brother Lazarus that was ill. So the sisters sent this message to him: "Please, Master, your dear friend is ill." "This illness," Jesus said on receiving the news, "will not result in death. No, it is to promote the glory of God. Through it the Son of God is to be glorified."

Now Jesus loved Martha and her sister and Lazarus. So, when he learned that he was ill, he tarried, it is true, for two days in the place where he was; but after that space of time he said to the disciples: "Let us go back into Judea." "Rabbi," the disciples said to him, "only recently the Jews wanted to stone you to death, and you mean to go back there again?" Jesus answered: "Are there not twelve hours to the day? As long as a man walks in the day time, he does not stumble, because he sees the light of this world. But when a man walks in the night time, he stumbles, because he has no light to guide him."

After saying this, he paused, and then continued: "Lazarus, our friend, has fallen asleep. Well, then, I will go and wake him from his sleep." "Master," the disciples said to him, "if he has fallen asleep, he will be all right." But Jesus had spoken of his death, whereas they imagined he had referred to the restfulness of sleep. Jesus now told them plainly: "Lazarus is dead. For your sake I am glad I was not there, so that you may believe. Come now; let us go to him." Here Thomas, called the Twin, said to his fellow disciples: "Let us go along and die with him."

When Jesus arrived, he found that Lazarus had already been four days in the tomb. Bethany was near Jerusalem, about two miles away; and many Jews had called on Martha and Mary to express their sympathy with them in the loss of their brother. As soon as Martha heard that Jesus was coming, she went to meet him, while Mary remained at home. Martha said to Jesus: "Master, if you had been here, my brother would not have died. And even now I know that whatever you ask of God, God will grant you." Jesus replied: "Your brother will rise again." "I know," Martha said to him, "he will rise again at the resurrection on the last day." "I am the resurrection and the life," Jesus said to her; "he who believes in me will live even if he dies; and no one that lives and believes in me shall be dead forever. Do you believe this?" "Yes, Master," she replied; "I firmly believe that you are the Messias, the Son of God, who was to come into the world."

With this, she returned and called her sister Mary privately. "The Master is here and asks for you," she said. As soon as Mary heard this, she rose quickly and went to meet him. Jesus had not yet entered the village, but was still at the spot where Martha had gone to meet him. Then the Jews who were with her in the house to offer their sympathy, on seeing Mary rise hurriedly and go out, followed her, supposing she was going to the tomb, there to give vent to her tears. When Mary came where Jesus was, she threw herself down at his feet as soon as she saw him, and said to him: "Master, if you had been here, my brother would not have died." She was weeping; and weeping, too, were the Jews who accompanied her. The sight of them stirred Jesus deeply and shook his inmost soul. "Where have you laid him to rest?" Jesus asked. "Come, and see, Master," they replied. Jesus burst into tears; and the Jews remarked: "Look, how dearly he loved him!" But some of them said: "He opened the eyes of the blind man; was he not able to prevent this man's death?"

Then Jesus, his inmost soul shaken again, made his way to the tomb. It was a cave, and a stone lay against the entrance. "Remove the stone," Jesus said. "Master," Martha, the dead man's sister, said to him, "his body stinks by this time; he has been dead four days." "Did I not tell you," replied Jesus, "that, if you have faith, you will see the glory of God?" So they removed the stone. Then Jesus lifted up his eyes and said: "Father, I thank you for listening to me. For myself, I knew that you always hear me; but I said it for the sake of the people surrounding me, that they might believe that I am your ambassador."

Having said this, he cried out in a strong voice: "Lazarus, come forth!" And he who had been dead came forth, wrapped hand and foot with bands, and his face muffled with a scarf. Jesus said to them: "Unwrap him and let him go."

Now many of the Jews — those who had called on Mary and witnessed what he did — believed in him; some of them, however, went to see the Pharisees and told them what Jesus had done. Thereupon the chief priests and the Pharisees convened a meeting of the Supreme Council. "This man," they urged, "is giving many proofs of power! What, then, are we to do? If we let him go without interference, all the world will believe in him; and then the Romans will come and put an end to our rank and race alike."

One of them, however, Caiaphas, who was chief priest in that year, said to them: "You are not men of vision! Can even you not understand that it is to our advantage that one man should die for the people so that the whole nation may be saved from ruin?" In saying this, he was wiser than he knew; the truth is, being chief priest in that year, he revealed God's design that Jesus was to die for the whole nation; and not only was he to save the whole nation, but to unite in one body all the scattered children of God. On that day, accordingly, they passed a resolution to put him to death.

As a result, Jesus would no longer move freely among the Jews, but left the place and, retiring to a town called Ephraim in the region skirting the desert, tarried there with his disciples.

Jn 11:1–54

25. Anyone Who Welcomes You Welcomes Me

In the Gospels there are several different relationships to Jesus and to His mission which are illustrated. Jesus preached to everyone that they must become perfect as their heavenly Father, God, is perfect. He also told some men to join Him in His special way of life as a traveling preacher. He told everyone to put love of God ahead of love for other persons but to practice love of others as love of God. But He called some people to actually leave their other works and loves to be with Him.

During His entire public life Jesus traveled with, and lived with, a group of twelve men whom He had chosen. He began the setting-apart of these men while John was still baptizing at the Jordan River. Then John pointed Jesus out to Andrew, who brought Peter to him. These brothers, Peter and Andrew, were fishermen. They seem, then, to have returned from the Jordan to northern Palestine to the Sea of Galilee to fish. There Jesus found them again and told them to follow Him.

Jesus also invited two other fishermen from that place to join him. These were the brothers James and John, sons of Zebedee. Later Jesus saw a man named Matthew (or Levi) sitting by the customs house and he said to him, "follow me." One by one Jesus selected this core following of twelve men. They are called the apostles.

Other people joined Jesus as well, both men and women. These appear casually in the Gospels so that it is hard to form a complete picture of the group which moved about together.

There is reason to think that they generally camped out. Jesus once said He was more homeless than the foxes who have their dens. At another place the Gospels mention that although Jesus spent His days preaching in the temple in Jerusalem, at night He went outside the town to the Mount of Olives. He spent many nights on mountains in the wilderness. The apostles fished and moved around on the Sea of Galilee at night. We get a picture of an outdoor life such as we can find the natives of some of the warmer underdeveloped countries living today. Luke gives us one glimpse of this fairly large group of rustic pilgrims:

> There followed a period of wandering about, during which he preached in town after town, in village after village, and announced the Good News of the kingdom of God. He was accompanied by the Twelve, as well as by certain women who had been cured of evil spirits and infirmities: Mary, surnamed the Magdalen, out of whom seven demons had been driven; Joanna, the wife of Chuza, Herod's manager, Susanna, and many others. These women were ministering to the company out of their own means.
>
> Lk 8:1–3

Just as it is clear from the Gospels (unless we follow the very involved analyses of some scripture scholars) that Jesus knew He was to die, it is also very clear that He meant His mission to be continued by other people. Although Jesus did not plan an organization, or what we call a Church, He did send men out into society in His name. He sent the apostles, a larger group of disciples, and some individuals on various special missions. He told his apostles (after His death and resurrection, when there were only eleven of them), "Go out to the whole world; proclaim the Good News to all creation."

When Jesus had finally left the earth Peter took the initiative and proposed that a replacement be chosen for Judas, the dead betrayer, so Matthias was selected by lot. Acts shows that the twelve apostles had a unique role and that they had no alternates or successors in their role. We even meet them in the Book of Revelation, or Apocalypse, in the description of the heavenly Jerusalem: "The city walls stood on twelve foundation stones, each one of which bore the name of one of the twelve apostles of the Lamb (Jesus)."

One of the most complete pictures which scripture gives of Jesus' life and relationship with the apostles is, curiously, an appendix about one of Jesus' post-resurrection appearances. This addition, chapter 21 in John's Gospel, also brings out Peter's unique role. Here is the entire, exceptionally vivid, final episode:

> On a later occasion Jesus showed himself again to the disciples, this time by the Lake of Tiberias. He did so under the following circumstances: Simon Peter, Thomas called the Twin, Nathanael of Cana in Galilee, the sons of Zebedee, and two others of his disciples, happened to be together. Simon Peter said to them: "I am going fishing." "We will go along with you," they replied. So they set out and got into the boat, and during that entire night they caught nothing. But just as day was breaking, Jesus stood on the beach. The disciples did not know, however, that it was Jesus. "Well, lads," Jesus said to them, "you have no fish there, have you?" "No," they replied. "Cast your net to the right of the boat," he said to them, "and you will find something." So they cast it, and now they were not strong enough to haul it up into the boat because of the great number of fish in it. Then the disciple whom Jesus loved said to Peter: "It is the Master!" No sooner did Simon Peter learn that it was the Master than he girt his upper garment about him — for he was wearing little — and plunged into the lake. Meanwhile the other disciples came on in the boat — for they were not far from the shore, only about two hundred yards — dragging along the net full of fish.
>
> When they had come ashore, they noticed hot embers on the ground, with fish lying on the fire and bread. Jesus said to them: "Bring some of the fish you caught just now." So Simon Peter boarded the boat and hauled the net upon the beach. It was full of fish, one hundred and fifty-three in all, and in spite of the great number the net did not break. "Come, now," Jesus said to them, "and have breakfast." Not one of his disciples could find it in his heart to ask him, "Who are you?" They knew it was the Master. Then Jesus approached, took the bread in his hands, and give them of it. He did the same with the fish. This was now the third time that Jesus showed himself to the disciples after he had risen from the dead.
>
> After they had breakfasted, Jesus said to Simon Peter: "Simon, son of John, do you love me more than these others do?" "Yes, my Master," he replied; "you know that I really love you." "Then," Jesus said to him, "feed my lambs." He asked

him a second time: "Simon, son of John, do you love me?"
"Yes, Master," he replied, "you know that I really love you."
"Then," he said to him, "be a shepherd to my sheep." For the
third time he put the question to him: "Simon, son of John,
do you really love me?" It grieved Peter that he had asked
him the third time: "Do you really love me?" and he replied:
"Master, you know everything; you know that I really love
you!" "Then," Jesus said to him, "feed my sheep. I tell you
the plain truth: when you were young, you used to put on
your own belt and go where you wished; but when you grow
old, you will stretch out your arms for someone else to gird
you and carry you where you have no wish to go." He said
this to signify the kind of death by which he was to glorify
God. And having said this, he said to him: "Follow me."

Turning round, Peter saw the disciple whom Jesus loved
following them, the same who at the supper had been resting
against his bosom and had asked: "Master, who is it that is
going to betray you?" So, at sight of him, Peter said to Jesus:
"And what about him, Master?" Jesus replied: "If I want him
to stay till I return, what difference does this make to you?
Your duty is to follow me." Accordingly, the report became
current among the brethren that that disciple was not going
to die. But Jesus had not said to him that he was not to die,
but simply: "If I want him to stay till I return, what difference
does this make to you?"

This is the disciple who is both the witness of these facts
and the recorder of these facts; and we know that his testimony
is true. There are, however, many other things that Jesus did
— so many that, should they all be recorded in full detail, the
world is not likely to hold all the volumes that would have
to be written.

Jn 21:1–25

The apostolic life

In the Gospel of Matthew, which is arranged by topics of
thought rather than by the sequence of events, chapter ten is all
about Jesus' instructions to the twelve apostles. The word "apostle"
means "one sent." This chapter shows how the messengers of Jesus
are sent as messengers from God. They are dependent for their
daily bread in the way we saw that Jesus proposed in the Lord's
Prayer and in His talk about the lilies of the field:

He then called to him his twelve apostles and gave them power to drive out unclean spirits, as well as power to heal any disease and any infirmity. The names of the twelve apostles are as follows:

First, Simon, surnamed Peter;
then Andrew, his brother;
James, the son of Zebedee,
and his brother John;
Philip and Bartholomew;
Thomas and the tax collector Matthew;
James, the son of Alpheus, and Thaddeus;
Simon the Cananaean;
and Judas Iscariot,
the same that eventually betrayed him.

These Twelve Jesus sent on a missionary tour, after giving them the following instructions:

"Do not turn aside into Gentile territory, and enter no Samaritan town. Instead, go to the lost sheep of the house of Israel. As you go along, preach on this text: 'The kingdom of heaven is close at hand.' Attend to the sick; raise the dead; make lepers clean; drive out demons. Gratis you have received; gratis you must give. Do not procure pocket money, whether gold or silver or copper; or a traveling bag, or an extra tunic, or sandals, or a staff. After all, a laborer is entitled to his support.

"Once you enter a town or village, search out a worthy citizen, and in his home make your headquarters till you leave that locality. On entering the house, salute it, and in case the household is responsive, your blessing will alight on it; if it is not responsive, your blessing will be no loss to you. But should the people not make you welcome and not listen to your preaching, leave that house or town, and shake the dust off your feet."

Mt 10:1–15

Jesus told His disciples that they would be persecuted. He told them that He, Himself, was going to suffer and die. At first they rejected this idea entirely. It is interesting to see, through the sequence of events in the Gospels and in Acts, how they gradually grew to understand and accept this idea of suffering as central to Jesus' mission and central to their own. The record of Peter's conversion in this respect is given with amusing details: at first Peter tells Jesus to stop talking such nonsense, later he denies knowing Jesus, after Pentecost he stands up to officials and tells them he couldn't care less what they say since his obedience is directed to God, and when he is imprisoned and released by an angel in the night he is so far from his fearful earlier self that the whole incident takes on an air of comedy. This last incident is in the Acts of the Apostles. But we are still talking about the early times in Jesus' public life. Then Jesus talked of suffering but His followers did not believe Him. We read in Luke:

> But while all expressed admiration for all he did he said to his disciples: "Let what I now say to you sink deep into your ears; the Son of Man is destined to be betrayed into the hands of men." They could not see the drift of his remark; it was a mystery to them, and they failed to grasp it. Besides, they were too timid to ask him what he meant.
>
> Lk 9:44-45

The major part of Jesus' instruction to His apostles given in Matthew is designed to prepare the apostles to suffer and stand up confidently in the face of persecution. Here are parts of Jesus' instruction:

> "Beware of your fellow men; they will try to hand you over to courts of justice and to flog you in their synagogues; you will even be brought before governors and kings for my sake. It will be your chance to testify to Jew and Gentile. But once handed over, do not be uneasy about how or what to speak; for at that moment the words will be put into your mouth. In fact, not you are then the speakers; no, the Spirit of your Father is then the Speaker inspiring you."
>
> "No pupil is above his teacher, and no slave above his master. It is enough for a pupil to be treated like his teacher, and for a slave, like his master. If people called the head of the household 'Beelzebul,' how much more so the members of his family!"
>
> "Do not fear people that kill the body, but have no power to kill the soul; rather, fear him who has power to ruin both body and soul in the infernal pit. Do not two sparrows sell for a penny? And yet, not one of them can drop dead to the

ground without the consent of your Father. As for yourselves, the very hairs of your head have all been numbered. Away, then, with all fear; you are more precious than whole flocks of sparrows.

"In short, everyone who acknowledges me before the world will, in turn, be acknowledged by me before my Father in heaven; but he who disowns me before the world will himself be disowned by me before my Father in heaven.

"Do not suppose that it is my mission to shed peace upon the earth; it is not my mission to shed peace but to unsheath the sword."

Mt 10:17–20, 24–25, 28–34

Matthew concludes this chapter on the mission of the apostles with two well known, often repeated, sayings of Jesus. Jesus told His followers that anyone who welcomed them was welcoming Him and also the God who sent Him. He said that anyone who gave so much as a cup of cold water to His disciples was certain to be rewarded.

The dispute among the twelve

On the whole the twelve apostles seem to have gotten along with each other remarkably well. But there was one unpleasant incident which caused a quarrel among them. In one version the mother of James and John is an intermediary who speaks to Jesus on behalf of her sons. Mark's description of the incident leaves her out. On this occasion, again, Jesus brought out the idea that He was the suffering servant of whom Isaiah had spoken and that His followers were to be like Him in suffering:

Then James and John, the sons of Zebedee, approached him. "Rabbi," they said to him, "we would like you to do for us whatever we ask of you." He replied: "What would you like me to do for you?" They said to him: "Give us a seat, one at your right, the other at your left, in your glory." "You do not realize what you are asking," Jesus said to them; "can you drink the cup that I am to drink, and be baptized with the baptism with which I am to be baptized?" "We can," they replied. Then Jesus said to them: "Yes, you shall drink the cup that I am to drink, and be baptized with the baptism with which I am to be baptized; but as for a seat at my right or my left,

[163]

that is not in my power to assign except to those for whom it has been reserved."

When the other ten heard of this incident, they gave way to indignation at James and John. Jesus called them into his presence and said to them: "You know that the distinguished rulers of the Gentiles lord it over their subjects, and that their princes tyrannize over them. That is not your way! On the contrary, he who would be a prince among you must be your servant, and he who would be a leader among you must be the slave of everyone. Why, even the Son of Man did not come into the world to be served but to serve and to give his life as a ransom for many."

Mk 10:35–45

Other disciples and friends of Jesus

Besides the twelve apostles, Jesus sent a group of seventy-two of His followers on a mission. Their instructions were the same as those of the apostles. These missions of his followers were not of very long duration.

The disciples seem to have come and gone from Jesus' camp. Even the apostles seem to have taken days off, or nights, to fish. While the whole group of Jesus' followers camped in the countryside when it was together, it appears that when groups were not too large they lived wherever they found hospitality. There is mention of time spent at the house of Matthew and with Peter's relatives. The one thing that is clear is that Jesus and His followers were not separated from ordinary people or ordinary life except briefly.

Jesus had a large following of disciples. From this group He selected an in-group of twelve to be the intimate associates of his mission and to continue it after his death. Outside these, so to speak, concentric circles, He had other friends and followers. With some of these people who were not a part of His missionary group, Jesus seems to have had extremely close and warm relationships. His friendship with the family at Bethany was as deep as His friendship with the twelve, to judge from scripture. Not only was His affection for Mary of Magdala very deep, but Jesus even appeared to her first after his resurrection and made her His special emmisary. However, she does not seem to have been one of the members of his traveling apostolic band.

While Jesus set a life-style for His apostolic groups on their missionary journies, and condemned the pursuit of riches and preoccupation with security and worldly "treasures," He never seems to have intended everyone to have the same relationship to His mission or the same life-style. Jesus told some people to follow Him and some people not to follow Him, but to return to their homes. Many of the people whom Jesus said were saved or blessed, such as the widow who lived on the pagan coastland, Zachaeus who climbed the tree to see him, and the Roman centurion who had such deep faith, were not told to follow Him. In fact, although Jesus was always criticizing the Scribes, there was one member of this group whom Jesus praised and of whom He said, "you are not far from the kingdom of heaven."

Jesus said bluntly whom He considered to be "with Him." "My mother and my brothers are those who hear the word of God and put it into practice." Jesus spoke of the coming of judgment. He did not say that the elect were those set apart by life-style or missionary activity, but "of two men in the fields one is taken; of two women at the millstone grinding, one is taken, one left."

On the other hand, Jesus did tell His followers that they would be rewarded:

> Then Peter remarked: "We, you see, have given up our possessions and become your followers." "I tell you with assurance," he said to them, "no one gives up home, or parents, or brothers, or wife, or children, for the sake of the kingdom of God, but receives many times as much in this world and eternal life in the world to come."
>
> Lk 18:28–30

These two aspects of Jesus' call to His followers have to be both kept in mind. The Master called *everyone* to perfection and to the reward of virtue, and He called *some people,* apparently on a purely individual basis, to an extraordinary missionary life, both with temporary and permanent missions.

26. The First Christian Activities

Faith in Jesus, or the religion we call "Christianity" spread very rapidly around the Mediterranean world during the first twenty-five years after the resurrection. In telling about this growth, Luke brings out very forcefully the continuing activity of the Holy Spirit. He tells us about the transition from association with Jesus, the unique person who was what is called a "prophet" in religion, to a religious group or church. In the church people attempt to follow the ideas which the prophet taught and to become like him. In a church people together have to solve their problems. They can no longer simply go to ask the prophet and source of their faith for he is no longer present with them in human form. They have to ask each other. Luke tells us about the problems of the first followers of Jesus, or rather, their one main problem.

The first Christians had what we might call an identity crisis. They were puzzled by a problem not altogether unlike the problems Christians face today. Today Christians are puzzled about their relation to "secular" society, to each other and to the Jewish people. The big problem of the first Christians was, how do we relate to the Jewish community?

In fact, Jesus, His mother Mary, the twelve apostles and all the original Christians were Jews. After Jesus had left them they were not at first sure whether all the followers of Jesus were meant to be Jews also. Should converts to Jesus be made Jews by circumcision? Should Christians obey all the Hebrew laws about clean and unclean foods? Should gentiles, that is, non-Jews, be admitted to the Christian community at all? Really it was a fantastic situation: these people who had started out in life to be fishermen, civil servants, artisans, or housewives suddenly found themselves thrown together and about a work they had never dreamed of. They hadn't even thought to ask Jesus some of the questions they now

[166]

needed to answer. How did the problems of the first Christians get solved?

It is intriguing to read the first part of Acts from the point of view of this problem of the relationship with Judaism. Not that the events recorded aren't interesting in themselves and for other reasons. But if we ask, how did this event, and that event, lead to the solution of the problem of the relationship with Judaism, then Luke's report seems very orderly and we can learn much about growth in the spirit of Jesus. Each event is like a step built upon the previous step.

Before he begins to show us how the Christians grew in self-knowledge, Luke summarizes Jesus' final days on earth. He tells us about Jesus' ascension. "They" are Jesus' disciples:

> So, when they had come together they asked him, "Lord, will you at this time restore the kingdom to Israel?"
>
> "It is not for you," he answered them, "to know the times or the dates which the Father has fixed by his own authority; but you shall receive power when the Holy Spirit comes upon you, and you shall be my witnesses in Jerusalem and in all Judea and Samaria and even to the very ends of the earth."
>
> After he had said this, he was lifted up before their eyes, and a cloud took him out of their sight. While they were gazing up to the sky as he went, at that moment two men stood beside them in white garments and said, "Men of Galilee, why do you stand looking up to the sky? This Jesus who has been taken up from you will come in the same way as you have seen him going into the sky."
>
> Acts 1:6–11

Then Luke tells us that the eleven apostles (remember Judas had betrayed Jesus and commited suicide so there were only eleven apostles left) — the eleven apostles, the women who traveled with them caring for them, and other disciples, were all staying together in an upper room. Jesus' mother Mary was a member of this group. They all spent their time in prayer and were of one mind.

Twelve foundation stones

Peter was inspired to propose that they choose a replacement for the dead betrayer, Judas. Without Judas the apostles numbered only eleven. The Israelites had had twelve founders: the twelve sons of Jacob, or Israel. The social organization of the chosen people was based on these twelve foundation stones. Did not Jesus choose twelve men? Peter said, we must fill up the number of the apostles from among those who have been followers of Jesus since John's baptism. Two of those present fulfilled this qualification. Lots were cast: Matthias was chosen over Barnabas to be the twelfth apostle.

Again they were twelve. Twelve what? Peter explained that they were witnesses of Jesus' resurrection. Now, what about the problem we chose to pursue. Don't you think that the establishing of this foundation group of twelve men already shows that Christian development is going to take the direction of a break with Judaism? The Israelites, or Jews, already had a foundation and did not need another. When a new foundation is built does this not show that the old is to be abandoned? What is going to be built on the foundation of the twelve apostles?

Fifty days have passed

The next event recorded in the Acts of the Apostles is what we call Pentecost. "Pentecost" is the name of a Jewish feast of thanksgiving which comes fifty days after the Passover feast. You remember that the Lord's Supper was a Passover meal. Now fifty unbelievable days have passed for Jesus' followers. They are together, possibly in the same room as that used for the Lord's Supper. Their thoughts are centered on Jesus.

Perhaps then John reminded his brethren of words he remembered Jesus to have said those fifty days ago:

> "If you love me, you will treasure my commandments. And I will ask the Father, and he will grant you another Advocate to be with you for all time to come, the Spirit of Truth! The world is incapable of receiving him, because it neither sees him nor knows him. You will know him, because he will make his permanent stay with you and in you.

Jn 14:15–17

What did Jesus mean by these words? Even at the time the apostles had been puzzled. One of them had said to Jesus:

> . . . "And what is the reason, Master, why you intend to manifest yourself to us and not to the world?" By way of

answer Jesus said to him: "Anyone who loves me will treasure my message, and my Father will love him, and we shall visit him and make our home with him. He who does not treasure my message does not love me; and, mind you, the message you have heard is not mine but the Father's, whose ambassador I am!

"I have told you all this while I am still lingering in your midst; but the Advocate, the Holy Spirit, whom the Father will send in my name, will teach you everything, and refresh your memory of everything I have told you."

Jn 14:22–26

Still the disciples did not know the day or the hour when these predictions were to be fulfilled. Neither did they know what the Holy Spirit, the Advocate, was going to be like to feel or see. Then the Spirit did come, and He came suddenly. What do you think Acts tells us about this event to which Jesus had given such importance? You will be surprised. The coming of the Spirit seems to be all in one short paragraph:

When the day of Pentecost had come, they were all together in one place. Suddenly there came a sound in the sky, as of a violent wind blowing, and it filled the whole house where they were staying. And there appeared to them tongues like fire which distributed themselves and settled on each one of them. They were all filled with the Holy Spirit and began to speak in other tongues, as the Holy Spirit prompted them to give utterance.

Acts 2:1–4

The great initial conversion

You see, the apostles and the authors of the biblical books just weren't interested in how it felt to be there. The whole importance and meaning of Pentecost is found in the activity which followed the giving of the Spirit. The first coming of the Spirit was but a moment in a continuous coming which is what all Christian history is about. The presence of the Spirit has consequences. It is an active force moving people in the world. This is what matters and this is what Luke tells us about:

Now there were staying at Jerusalem devout men of every nation. When this sound was heard, a crowd of them gathered and were bewildered, because each one heard his own language spoken by the apostles. Everybody was amazed and marveled, saying, "Look, are not all those who are speaking Galileans? How then does each of us hear his own native language? Parthians and Medes, and Elamites, and inhabitants of Mesopotamia, Judea and Cappadocia, Pontus and Asia, Phrygia and Pamphylia, Egypt and the districts of Libya and Cyrene, and visitors from Rome, Jews and Proselytes, Cretans and Arabians — we hear them declaring in our own languages the wonderful works of God."

They were all amazed and perplexed, saying to one another, "What does this mean?" Others said in mockery, "They are full of sweet wine."

But Peter, presenting himself with the Eleven, raised his voice and addressed them: "Men of Judea and all you who reside in Jerusalem, let me inform you of this, and give ear to my words. These men are not drunk, as you suppose, since it is only nine o'clock in the morning. But this is what was foretold by the prophet Joel:

'It shall happen in the last days, says God,
    that I will pour forth my Spirit on all mankind;
And your sons and daughters shall prophesy,
    and your young men shall see visions,
    and your old men shall dream dreams.
And on my slaves too and my handmaids
    in those days will I pour forth my Spirit,
    and they shall prophesy.
I will also show wonders in the heavens above
    and signs on the earth below,
    blood and fire and a cloud of smoke.
The sun shall be turned into darkness
    and the moon into blood,
Before the day of the Lord comes,
    the great and manifest day.
And it shall happen
that whoever calls on the name of the Lord
    shall be saved.'

"Men of Israel, hear these words. Jesus of Nazareth was a man accredited to you by God through miracles and wonders and signs, which God did through him in your midst, as you yourselves know. When he was delivered up by the settled purpose and foreknowledge of God, you crucified and slew him by the hands of wicked men. But God has raised him up, having put an end to the pangs of death, because it was not possible that death should hold him. For David says of him:

'I saw the Lord before me always,
because he is at my right hand lest I be shaken.
This is why my heart has made merry
and my tongue has rejoiced.
Even my flesh will rest in hope,
because you will not abandon my soul to death
and you will not let your Holy One see decay.
You have made known to me the path that leads to life;
You will fill me with joy in your presence.'

"Brothers, we are permitted to speak with firm assurance to you of the patriarch David who died and was buried. His tomb is with us to this day. Therefore, since he was a prophet and knew that God had sworn to him with an oath that of his offspring one was to sit on his throne, he spoke with foreknowledge of the resurrection of the Christ, who was not abandoned to the grave, and whose flesh did not see decay. God has raised up this Jesus, and of that fact we are all witnesses."

Acts 2:5–32

Peter ended his speech by saying that "for this reason the whole House of Israel can be certain that God has made this Jesus whom you crucified both Lord and Christ." The people listening to Peter were converted in their hearts. How did they respond? They asked what they could *do*. Peter did not tell them to go to the Jewish temple and offer sacrifice or anything that was part of the Hebrew worship. He was thinking independently of Judaism even if he did not yet quite realize it. This is what Peter told them:

"Have a change of heart and mind . . . and be baptized everyone of you in the name of Jesus Christ for the remission of your sins: then you will receive the gift of the Holy Spirit. The promise is meant for you and for your children and for all who are afar off, for all whom the Lord our God may call to himself."

Acts 2:38–39

They were convinced. They asked for baptism. Acts reports that 3000 persons were added that day to the number of the disciples of Jesus.

Luke also tells us, in an odd little summary at this place in Acts, that the Christians had already developed a pattern of life. They were sharing their goods and meeting to re-enact the Lord's Supper in their homes. At the same time they were still leading a Jewish life and praying together in the temple.

The next part of Acts is about miracles performed mostly by Peter. These miracles led to the arrest of Peter and John. They were freed and re-arrested.

That the pattern of community life became clearer is shown in the next section. Deacons are chosen as a first subdivision of work. Then one of these deacons, Stephen, was stoned to death. He was the first of many men and women killed because of their faith in Jesus. Much of this development has to do with our problem question, but since, if we tried to talk about every relevant happening in Acts, we would never finish, we are going to skip to the event which proved crucial for the solution of our problem question. This event finally settled the relationship between Christianity and Judaism as the apostle Peter faced it. Later, at Jerusalem, the Church agreed to accept his insight.

When Peter saw that God gave the same Spirit to the pagan Cornelius that He gave to the Jews, he was convinced of the universality of Christianity. Christian converts need not be or become Jews. God's dealings with Cornelius witness to God's rejection of exclusiveness. No man, as Peter at last realized, is to be called "profane" in the sense of not fit for God or unclean.

Despite this revelation, and many other specific ones, and the whole of Jesus' teachings there have been believers in Christ who called other believers in Christ condemned, or have tried to force them to believe their way, or have condemned other peoples like the followers of Islam, or imagined that God's children of the Eastern religions were abandoned, or His primitive tribes. The history of Cornelius' conversion is actually very complex and so to speak two-sided. It is an account, both of conversion, and of the realization that God's grace is given to the unconverted.

Now that the improvement of transportation has made all the

peoples of the world close neighbors it is especially important that devout Christians learn what their religion teaches them about the universality of God's activity. Perhaps today's Christians can, like Peter, arrive at a new level of growth in Christ Jesus, by absorbing the lesson God taught through Cornelius:

Now there was in Caesarea a man named Cornelius, a centurion of the cohort called Italian. He was devout and God-fearing, as was all his household. He gave alms generously to the people and prayed to God continually. About three o'clock in the afternoon he perceived distinctly in a vision an angel of God enter his house and say to him, "Cornelius!" Gazing at the angel in awe he said: "What is it, Lord?" "Your prayers," replied the angel, "and your alms have gone up and been remembered in the sight of God. And now send men to Joppa and fetch Simon, surnamed Peter: he is lodging with Simon a tanner, whose house is by the seaside." When the angel who had spoken to him had departed, Cornelius called two of his household servants and a God-fearing soldier from among his personal attendants, and after telling them the whole story sent them to Joppa.

Now the next day, while they were still on their journey and were just drawing near to the city, Peter went up to the roof about noon to pray. He became very hungry and wanted something to eat. While food was being prepared, he fell into an ecstasy, and saw the sky opened and a receptacle descending like a great sheet, let down by the four corners to the earth. In it were all the four-footed beasts and creeping things of the earth and the birds of the air. A voice came to him, "Rise, Peter, kill and eat." "Far be it from me Lord," said Peter, "for never did I eat anything common or unclean." A second time a voice came to him, "What God has cleansed, do not call common." Now this happened three times, when forthwith the receptacle was taken up into the sky.

Now while Peter was still perplexed as to what the vision he had seen might mean, just then the men sent by Cornelius stood at the door, inquiring for Simon's house, and calling out to ask whether Simon, surnamed Peter, was staying there. While Peter was pondering over the vision, the Spirit said to him, "At this moment three men are looking for you. Rise, therefore, go down and depart with them without hesitation, for I have sent them." So Peter went down to the men and said, "Here I am, the man you are asking for. What is the reason for your coming?" "Cornelius," they answered him, "a centurion, a just and God-fearing man, who enjoys a good reputation with the whole nation of the Jews, has been directed by a holy angel to fetch you to his house and to hear a message from you." So he invited them in and entertained them.

The next day he set out and went with them, accompanied by some of the brothers from Joppa. The following day he reached Caesarea. Now Cornelius was waiting for them with a number of his relatives and intimate friends whom he had invited. As Peter entered, Cornelius met him and fell at his feet in reverence. But Peter raised him up, saying, "Get up, I myself also am a man." As he talked with Cornelius, he went in and found many assembled, and said to them, "You know it is not permissible for a Jew to associate with a foreigner or to visit him, but God has shown me that I should not call any man common or unclean. Therefore I came without hesitation when I was summoned. I ask, therefore, why you have sent for me?"

"Three days ago at this very hour," replied Cornelius, "I was praying in my house at three o'clock in the afternoon, and suddenly a man stood before me in shining garments who said, 'Cornelius, your prayer has been heard and your alms have been remembered in the sight of God. Send therefore to Joppa and summon Simon, surnamed Peter. He is lodging in the house of Simon, a tanner, by the sea.' Accordingly at once I sent for you, and you have very kindly come. Now, therefore, we are all present before God to hear whatever the Lord has commanded you."

Peter began to address them: "Now I really understand that God shows no partiality, but in every nation the man that fears him and does what is right is acceptable to him. He sent his word to the children of Israel, proclaiming the Good News of peace through Jesus Christ, who is Lord of all. You know what took place throughout Judea. Jesus of Nazareth began in Galilee after the baptism preached by John. You know how God anointed him with the Holy Spirit and with power, and he went about doing good and healing all who were in the power of the devil because God was with him. We are witnesses of all that he did in the country of the Jews

[174]

and in Jerusalem. Yet they killed him, hanging him on a cross. But God raised him up on the third day and caused him to be plainly seen, not by all the people, but by witnesses designated beforehand by God, that is, by us, who ate and drank with him after he had risen from the dead. Jesus also charged us to preach to the people and to bear witness that it is he who has been appointed by God to be judge of the living and the dead. To him all the prophets bear witness that through his name all who believe in him may receive forgiveness of sins."

While Peter was still speaking these words, the Holy Spirit came on all who were listening to his message. The Jewish faithful, Peter's companions, were amazed, because the gift of the Holy Spirit had also been poured forth on the Gentiles, for they heard them speaking in tongues and magnifying God. Then Peter made the decision: "Can anyone refuse the baptism of water to these people, seeing that they have received the Holy Spirit just as we did?" So he ordered them to be baptized in the name of Jesus Christ. Then they besought him to stay on there for a few days.

Acts 10:1–48

27. To the Whole World

We have seen that Stephen, one of the first seven deacons, was stoned to death. After His death, persecution of Jesus' followers began in earnest. The disciples began to scatter. Some went to Antioch, an important city on the Mediterranean coast. There the independence of the new religion was recognized. Jesus' followers began to be called "Christians." Christ means "anointed"; Christians are the followers of Jesus, the anointed one.

In Jerusalem the apostle James was put to death. Peter was imprisoned, but he was rescued by an angel. The story has both comic and tragic details: the Christians were praying at Mark's house, perhaps for Peter's release, but when Peter arrived at the door the girl who answered his knock got so excited that she ran to tell everyone without letting Peter in. As for the poor guards, they were executed for letting Peter escape. You can read about this in Acts, chapter 12.

Persecution led to the extension of Christianity. Wherever they fled the followers of Jesus made new converts. Christian communities sprang up all over the Roman empire and to the East as far as India. We are told very little about these new converts, but one unusual conversion proved especially significant. This man who was converted had been bent on extending the persecution of the followers of Jesus. He set out for Damascus for this purpose:

> But Saul, still breathing threats of death against the disciples of the Lord, went to the high priest, and asked him for letters to the synagogues at Damascus, so that, if he found any men or women belonging to the Way, he might bring them in bonds to Jerusalem. During his journey, it happened, as he was approaching Damascus, that suddenly a light from the

sky flashed round about him, and falling to the ground, he heard a voice saying to him, "Saul, Saul, why do you persecute me?" "Who are you, Lord?" he asked. Jesus replied, "I am Jesus whom you are persecuting. Arise and go into the city, and you will be told what you must do." Meanwhile his traveling companions remained speechless. They heard the voice but saw no one. Then Saul arose from the ground, and although his eyes were open, he could see nothing. So leading him by the hand, they brought him into Damascus. For three whole days he could not see, neither did he eat or drink.

Now there was in Damascus a disciple named Ananias, to whom the Lord said in a vision, "Ananias!" "Here I am, Lord," he answered. The Lord said to him, "Arise and go to the street called Straight and ask at the house of Judas for a man of Tarsus named Saul, who at this very moment is praying." (Saul saw a man named Ananias enter and lay his hands on him that he might recover his sight.) Ananias, however, objected, "Lord, I have heard from many a person about this man, how much evil he has done to your saints at Jerusalem. Even here he has authority from the high priest to arrest all who invoke your name." "Go," the Lord commanded him, "for this man is my chosen instrument, to carry my name among nations and their kings and among the children of Israel as well. I myself will show him how much he must suffer for my name."

So Ananias departed and entered the house. As he laid his hands on Saul he said, "Brother Saul, the Lord has sent me — Jesus, who appeared to you on your journey — that you may recover your sight and be filled with the Holy Spirit." Immediately there fell from Saul's eyes something likes scales, he recovered his sight, arose, and was baptized. Then after taking some food, he regained his strength.

Now for some days he lived with the disciples at Damascus. Without delay he began to preach Jesus as the Son of God in the synagogues.

Acts 9:1–20

Paul of Tarsus

Who was this Saul, also called Paul? He was a Hebrew from the Roman city of Tarsus, in modern Turkey. He studied the Mosaic Law under a famous Rabbi in Jerusalem. After his conversion to

Christ Jesus he dedicated the rest of his life to the gospel message. He traveled without ceasing around the Mediterranean world. He was killed in Rome under the Emperor Nero.

Paul is called the "apostle to the gentiles." Most of the letters included in the Bible are by Paul. He wrote them to the Christian churches he founded, or else to Christians he planned to visit. Scholars debate whether he wrote all of these long letters; maybe he did and maybe he didn't. A great part of the theoretical, organizational, and doctrinal development of Christianity has been based on the writings by (or attributed to) Paul. Some of this development is very uncritical and does not distinguish between the new man who "put on Jesus Christ" and the old man who knew the Mosaic Law inside out. Paul himself distinguished what Jesus taught from what he, Paul, thought, or recommended as a good solution to a particular problem. Paul is a model for the leaders of the Christian people: he knew what Jesus revealed and what Jesus had not said anything about, and when he himself had to make decisions based on circumstances and the signs of the times in the Spirit of Jesus, he made them fearlessly in his own name and called them his own, not those of Jesus.

Few have equalled Paul as a commentator on Jesus. But this is not his first strength. Paul's work is the first large scale application of Jesus' teachings to the problems of daily life, at least so far as we know. From this point of view his letters especially are invaluable. His way of going about applying Jesus' ideas is relevant today, even if all his solutions to his problems are not.

Paul's letters are masterpieces. He wrote some of the most exciting letters ever written, deeply exciting. Do you believe me? See what you think of this bit of self-defense Paul sent to the Christians of the decadent fun city of Corinth:

> I repeat, let no one think me foolish. But if so, then regard me even as such, that I may also boast a little. What I am saying with this assurance in boasting, I am not saying in keeping with the Lord's example, but as a fool. Since many boast for purely human reasons, I too will boast. Having so much common sense, you gladly put up with those that have none! For example, you tolerate it if a man enslaves you, or preys upon you, or makes away with your possessions, or is over-

weening, or slaps you in the face! I must confess to my shame:
it is to be believed that we have been too weak. But in whatever respect anyone has shown boldness, I too show the same
boldness. I know that I am speaking foolishly. Are they Hebrews? So am I! Are they Israelites? So am I. Are they the
descendants of Abraham? So am I! Are they ministers of Christ?
I — to speak like a man out of his mind — surpass them by
reason of fatiguing labors more abundant, imprisonments more
frequent, lashings innumerable, many threats of death. From
the Jews five times I received forty lashes less one. Three
times I was scourged, once I was stoned, three times I suffered
shipwreck; a night and a day I was adrift on the high sea;
in frequent journeys on foot, in perils from floods, in perils
from robbers, in perils from my own nation, in perils from
the Gentiles, in perils in the city, in perils in the wilderness,
in perils on the sea, in perils from false brothers, in fatigue
and harship, in many sleepless nights, in hunger and thirst, in
fastings, often in cold and nakedness. Apart from these things,
there is my daily pressing anxiety, my solicitude for all the
congregations! Who is weak without my sympathizing with
his weakness? Who is led astray without my burning with
indignation?

If I must boast, I will boast of the things that show my
weakness. The God and Father of our Lord Jesus Christ, who
is blessed for evermore, knows that I do not lie. In Damascus
the ethnarch of King Aretas had stationed guards about the
city with the intention of having me arrested, but I was
lowered in a basket through a window in the wall, and escaped
his hands.

I am obliged to boast. Although there is nothing to be gained
by it, I will proceed to tell of the visions and revelations
granted me by the Lord. I know a man in Christ, who four-
teen years ago — whether in the body or out of the body I do
not know, God knows — this individual was caught up to the
third heaven. And I know that this person — whether in the
body or out of the body I do not know, God knows — was
caught up into paradise and heard unutterable utterances which
no man is permitted to repeat. Of such a man I will boast; but
as regards myself I will boast of nothing save my infirmities.
If I should wish to boast about myself, I would not be unrea-
sonable, since I should be telling the truth. But I forbear lest

[179]

any man should esteem me beyond what he sees me to be or hears from me on the basis of the surpassing grandeur of my revelations.

For this reason, lest I should be puffed up with vanity, there was given me a thorn for the flesh, a messenger of Satan to buffet me. Concerning this I three times besought the Lord that it might leave me. And he said to me, "My grace is sufficient for you, for my power is made perfectly evident in your weakness." Gladly, therefore, will I boast of my infirmities, that the power of Christ may spread a sheltering cover over me. For this reason I take delight for Christ's sake, in infirmities, in insults, in hardships, in persecutions, in distresses. For when I am weak, then I am strong.

2 Cor 1:16–12:10

This is where this little book must end. I am sorry to have to stop because so many fascinating stories and parables and adventures and deep thoughts about man and about God, which can be found in the Bible, have been left out. But you don't need to stop. You are a teen-ager, old enough and competent enough to read the Bible yourself. Perhaps the best place for you to begin is in the book of the Acts of the Apostles. And then browse back through the Synoptic Gospels. And then — you decide.

I hope that I have grown by writing this much for you, and that you have grown by reading it. And that we find ourselves moving toward God together, as Paul described this growth:

Whoever are led by the Spirit of God, they are the sons of God. Now you have not received a spirit of bondage so that you are again in fear, but you have received a spirit of adoption as sons, in virtue of which we cry, "Abba! Father!" The Spirit himself joins his testimony to that of our spirit that we are children of God. But if we are children, we are heirs also: heirs indeed of God and joint heirs with Christ, since we suffer with him that we may also be glorified with him.

I am sure that neither death, nor life, nor angels, nor principalities, nor things present, nor things to come, nor powers, nor height, nor depth, nor any other creature can separate us from God's love for us, which is in Christ Jesus our Lord.

Rom 8:14–17, 38–39